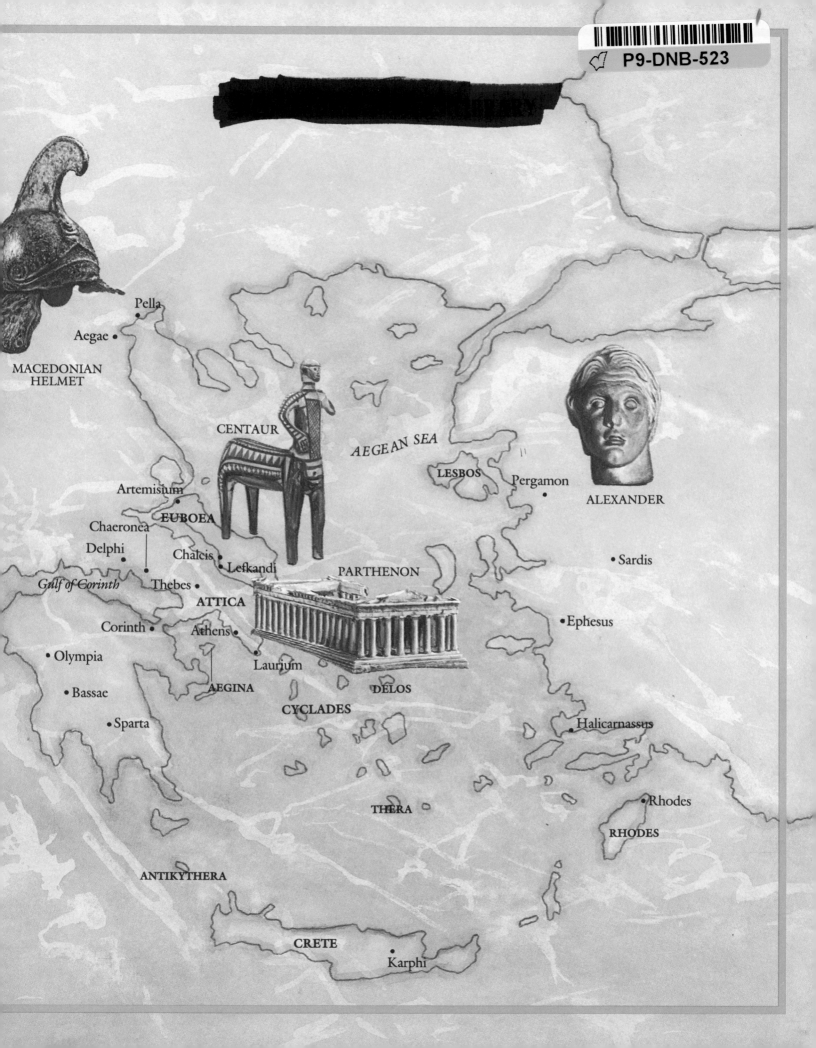

MACEDONIAN
HELMET

Pella

Aegae

CENTAUR

AEGEAN SEA

LESBOS

Pergamon

ALEXANDER

Artemisium

EUBOEA

Chaeronea

Delphi

Chalcis

Lefkandi

PARTHENON

Sardis

Gulf of Corinth

Thebes

ATTICA

Corinth

Athens

Olympia

Laurium

Ephesus

AEGINA

DELOS

Bassae

CYCLADES

Halicarnassus

Sparta

THERA

Rhodes

RHODES

ANTIKYTHERA

CRETE

Karphi

GREECE:
TEMPLES, TOMBS, & TREASURES

Time-Life Books is a division of TIME LIFE INC.

PRESIDENT and CEO: John M. Fahey Jr.
EDITOR-IN-CHIEF: John L. Papanek

TIME-LIFE BOOKS

MANAGING EDITOR: Roberta Conlan

Executive Art Director: Ellen Robling
Director of Photography and Research:
John Conrad Weiser
Senior Editors: Russell B. Adams Jr.,
Dale M. Brown, Janet Cave, Lee Hassig, Jim
Hicks, Robert Somerville, Henry Woodhead
Director of Technology: Eileen Bradley

PRESIDENT: John D. Hall

Vice President, Director of Marketing:
Nancy K. Jones
Vice President, New Product Development:
Neil Kagan
Director of Production Services: Robert N. Carr
Production Manager: Prudence G. Harris
Supervisor of Quality Control: James King

Editorial Operations
Production: Celia Beattie
Library: Louise D. Forstall
Computer Composition: Deborah G. Tait
(Manager), Monika D. Thayer, Janet
Barnes Syring, Lillian Daniels

**Library of Congress
Cataloging in Publication Data**
Greece: Temples, Tombs, & Treasures / by the
editors of Time-Life Books.
    p. cm.—(Lost civilizations)
Includes bibliographical references and index.
ISBN 0-8094-9020-X (trade)
ISBN 0-8094-9021-8 (library)
1. Greece—History—To 146 B.C.
2. Greece—Antiquities.
3. Excavations (Archaeology)—Greece.
I. Time-Life Books.   II. Series.
DF221.2.G75 1994
938—dc20   93-43570

LOST CIVILIZATIONS

SERIES EDITOR: Dale M. Brown
Administrative Editor: Philip Brandt George

Editorial staff for *Greece: Temples, Tombs, & Treasures*
Senior Art Director: Susan K. White
Art Director: Bill McKenney
Picture Editor: Marion Ferguson Briggs
Text Editors: Charles J. Hagner (principal),
Russell B. Adams Jr., Charlotte Anker, Jim
Lynch
Writer: Denise Dersin
Associate Editor/Research: Constance Contreras
Assistant Editor/Research: Mary Grace
Mayberry
Senior Copyeditor: Jarelle S. Stein
Picture Coordinator: David A. Herod
Editorial Assistant: Patricia D. Whiteford

Special Contributors: Anthony Allan, Douglas
Botting, Ellen Galford, Michael Thomas
Kerrigan, David S. Thomson (text); Tom
DiGiovanni, Eugenia S. Scharf, Lauren V.
Scharf, Ylann Schemm (research); Roy
Nanovic (index)

Correspondents: Elisabeth Kraemer-Singh
(Bonn), Christine Hinze (London), Christina
Lieberman (New York), Maria Vincenza
Aloisi (Paris), Ann Natanson (Rome).
Valuable assistance was also provided by
Mehmet Ali Kislali (Ankara); Maria Chadou,
Gregory Maniatis, Claire Milonas (Athens);
Gevene Hertz (Copenhagen); Judy Aspinall
(London); Elizabeth Brown (New York); Alex
Efty (Nicosia); Ann Wise (Rome); Theodor
Troev (Sophia); Mary Johnson (Stockholm);
Traudl Lessing (Vienna).

The Consultants:
Sir John Boardman, world renowned authority on ancient Greece, is Lincoln professor of classical archaeology and art at the University of Oxford and professor of ancient history at the Royal Academy of the Arts.

Robert Lindley Vann is professor of architecture at the University of Maryland, specializing in the history of Greek and Roman architecture. Dr. Vann also serves as director of the university's archaeological survey of ancient harbors in Turkey.

Barbara A. Barletta, associate professor of art history at the University of Florida, spent several years in Greece and Italy researching the architecture of the Greek colonies and is currently at work on a book about her findings.

For information on and a full description of any of the Time-Life Books series listed above, please call 1-800-621-7026 or write:
Reader Information
Time-Life Customer Service
P.O. Box C-32068
Richmond, Virginia 23261-2068

This volume is one in a series that explores the worlds of the past, using the finds of archaeologists and other scientists to bring ancient peoples and their cultures vividly to life.

Other volumes in the series include:

GREECE: TEMPLES, TOMBS, & TREASURES

By the Editors of Time-Life Books

TIME-LIFE BOOKS, ALEXANDRIA, VIRGINIA

CONTENTS

REDISCOVERING
A LAND
OF GIANTS

A few sherds of Greek pottery might not have seemed much of a find to their discoverers, and yet these would provide one of archaeology's most stirring moments when they were pieced together. The sherds had been dug up by a German team excavating on the Olympic plain, scene of the original Olympic Games and once the site of a magnificent temple dedicated in 460 BC to Zeus, father of the gods. The archaeologists had already spent five seasons, from 1954 through 1958, searching for remains of the workshop in which Phidias, the Athenian sculptor, had created his greatest—and by far and away his biggest—piece: an ivory and gold statue of the deity, which adorned the temple's interior.

Though little survives of the colossus, fragments of Phidias's sculptures for the Parthenon do *(opposite),* and they have ensured Phidias's reputation as the finest sculptor of the classical world. No previous artist had succeeded in making humans appear so divine or deities so human. It was said in ancient times that Phidias alone had seen the exact image of the gods and revealed it to humankind.

Phidias depicted Zeus sitting on a throne, his feet resting on a stool decorated with lion reliefs. The sculptor set a crown of olive branches on the god's head and placed in his left hand a scepter topped by an eagle. The work—which was destroyed by fire in AD 462, after having been moved in the fourth century AD to

Full of flowing movement, a marble torso from the west pediment of Athens's Parthenon displays the revolutionary approach of its fifth-century BC sculptor. Not only did he render the garment naturalistically but also the body beneath it.

7

Constantinople—made such a powerful impression on those who saw it that authors of antiquity ranked it among the Seven Wonders of the World. The statue rose 40 feet, the height of a four-story building. Zeus's head loomed so close to the ceiling that special elevated viewing platforms had to be constructed along the temple walls for visitors, such as the geographer Strabo, who toured Olympia in the first century AD, to take in the god's massive proportions. "We have the impression," the Greek noted, "that if Zeus moved to stand up, he would unroof the temple."

Fairly obviously, a work of this size had to have been assembled on site, but exactly where the actual production of its many components had been carried out remained a mystery. Digging in the area of a Byzantine church located west of the temple, the German team uncovered a pit for casting bronze; lumps of modeling plaster; scraps of worked ivory, lead, bronze, and obsidian; and a number of discarded burins, chisels, and spatulas—all sure signs of artistic activity. More revealing was a series of terra-cotta molds shaped like drapery, over which gold sheets could have been hammered to form Zeus's flowing robes. Some of the molds were even inscribed with numbers, which the archaeologists believe corresponded to specific locations on the statue.

The Germans knew they had found a sculptor's workshop all right, but was it Phidias's? Then the sherds turned up. Assembled, they formed a common Athenian blackware mug on whose underside someone had etched a line of fifth-century BC Greek letters. Starting on one fragment and ending on another, the inscription read, "I belong to Phidias."

The find seemed too good to be true, but microscopic examination of the letters on the mug bottom confirmed they were indeed authentic, laying to rest suspicions that the inscription had been scratched in the clay by a modern hoaxer. Clearly, the archaeologists had reason to celebrate; after years of diligent scholarship and patient, methodical digging, they held in their hands a vessel that Phidias himself may have lifted to his lips, that the artist himself may even have marked as his own. The emotion of the moment seemed to erase the intervening 2,400 years.

That is the magic of archaeology. It can draw people long dead close, bring them back to life. Thanks to advances in excavation techniques and the use of advanced technologies at sites scattered

Presumably once held by Phidias himself, sculptor's bronze tools unearthed from an ancient trash heap at the site of his Olympia workshop are paired here with the base of a mug bearing his name found at the same site. Archaeologists were convinced of the inscription's authenticity when microscopic analysis demonstrated that the writing predated the break and thus had not been added to the vessel in modern times.

throughout the Greek world, more is now known about the ancient Greeks than ever, with many of the finds providing new insights that require revision of old thinking. Archaeologists at work on the Aegean island of Euboea, for instance, have uncovered evidence that its early residents, those who lived three millennia ago and were regarded by scholars as dwelling in an uncivilized and inward-looking dark age, enjoyed instead a rich life. They prospered as they exchanged goods with traders as far away as Cyprus and Phoenicia.

The wonder is that there should be anything more to discover about a people as seemingly well studied as the ancient Greeks. But as so often happens when the subjects themselves are no longer around to set the record straight, many myths and half-truths have grown up. Archaeology is now helping to correct some of these. There was even a time when the Greeks were nearly forgotten, when the lands they called their own disappeared behind a curtain as impenetrable as the one that divided modern Europe during the Cold War. Only with a revival of interest in classical learning did the Greeks reenter imaginations and then not always to their historical advantage—or the benefit of the monuments they left behind.

The passion for Greece and all things Greek set off a treasure hunt. Those who traveled there often sought to bring back some memento of the classical past. They were, however, by no means the first to be possessed by such desire. The Romans, who conquered Greece in the second century BC, regarded Greek works of art, initially at least, as legitimate spoils of war. When the general Lucius Aemilius Paulus, for instance, returned triumphant from a campaign in 168 BC, he brought with him no fewer than 250 cartloads of statues, paintings, and metal vases. In later years, a flourishing export trade developed, and ships that were heavily laden with art treasures set sail for Italy, where sculptors developed elaborate molding techniques to copy Greek works. Until the first shipwrecks containing Greek bronzes were found in this century *(pages 111-119),* Roman versions of the ancient works remained the primary means of appreciating Greek sculpture.

The vogue for statuary typified the veneration with which Rome came to regard the culture of the lands it had subdued. Indeed, the Roman poet Horace remarked that "Greece the captive enthralled her savage captor." Greek thought soon saturated Roman education and Roman letters. Even a new form of literature—the guidebook—developed under Greek influence.

9

One such work was the *Description of Greece,* by Pausanias, a Greek physician and geographer who lived in the second century AD. Though intended to cater to the needs of the travelers who thronged to Greece in the heyday of the Roman Empire, his book proved invaluable to tourists in subsequent ages as well. "When traveling in Greece," recommended a minister to the French king Louis XIV, 15 centuries later, "one should have Pausanias in hand in order to find the remarkable things that he found when he made this journey long ago, and with the same curiosity."

The ruins of Olympia lie exposed in a circa 1900 photograph that includes columns of the palestra, or wrestling school, in the foreground and those of the Temple of Hera in the background. Apparently destroyed by an earthquake and subsequently covered by mud, sand, and gravel brought by floods and landslides, Olympia has proved a particularly rich site for German archaeologists, who have been digging here since 1875.

Less than a century after Pausanias's death, barbarian tribes sacked Athens, and in AD 395 the Roman Empire was divided into eastern and western halves. Greece fell into the eastern, or Byzantine, portion and thus began more than 14 centuries in which it would be ruled from Constantinople. By then, however, the ancient culture was almost at an end, having been dealt its deathblow by the spread of Christianity. When the new faith became the orthodoxy of the empire, worship of the Greek gods was proscribed. The temples were closed, and even the Olympic Games, sacred to Zeus, were abolished, not to be revived for 16 centuries.

And so Greece sank into a long sleep. Although the Byzantine world escaped much of the devastation the barbarians inflicted on western Europe of the day, the country suffered nonetheless, becoming a forgotten backwater whose remaining monuments moldered unprotected. Readers in Constantinople still studied and admired the works of classic Greek authors, but knowledge of these was virtually lost in Europe. The few European voyagers who found their way to the antique lands came back with wild tales—that the stone Gorgon's head on the Athenian Acropolis had powers to sink approaching ships, or that the daughter of the great physician Hippocrates roamed about in the form of a dragon, beseeching men to kiss her so that she might resume human form.

When Europeans did arrive in numbers, they came not as explorers or scholars but as conquerors. In 1204 the troops of the Fourth Crusade, supposedly headed for the Holy Land to fight the infidel, instead seized and sacked Christian Constantinople and initiated thereby the breakup of the Byzantine Empire. The Pelo-

In an 1883 highly imaginative reconstruction, Phidias's lost statue of Zeus sits in splendor in the Olympia temple dedicated to the god. It was noted at the time by the Academy of Beaux Arts in Paris that the French artist "captured a view of reality that, if it is not reality itself, is at least a very close reality."

ponnese and Athens, then a duchy, became possessions of Frankish princes, while the Ionian and Aegean islands, Rhodes, Crete, and a few scattered outposts on the mainland fell into Venetian hands. Though the Byzantines won back control of Constantinople half a century later, Greece and its former domains remained weak and fragmented under largely foreign rulers.

By the time interest in the classical world reawakened with the first stirrings of the Renaissance, Greece was no more than a shadow of its former self. Poverty and roaming herds of voracious goats had reduced much of the country to a bandit-haunted wilderness of worn-out soil and deforested hillsides. The great temples and civic buildings of the past had mostly collapsed, and the landscape had become a rubble-strewn wasteland.

The renewed interest in Greece initially focused on classical

TEMPLE DE JVPITER
COVPE ~ TRANSVERSALE

TWISTS AND TURNS IN THE DIFFICULT ART OF RESTORING HELLENISTIC SCULPTURE

The power and energy of Greece's Hellenistic age is vividly expressed in its sculptures. Among its most dynamic is the Laocoön, unearthed near Rome during the Renaissance. This dramatic work shows the priest Laocoön and his sons being punished for having warned the citizens of Troy against the Trojan Horse. It is now thought to be a first-century AD marble copy by the Greek sculptors Agesander, Athenodorus, and Polydorus of a second-century BC Greek bronze. When it was discovered, the sculpture lacked several parts, including the priest's right arm, and subsequently underwent a series of restorations (*far right*). Then, in 1960, the limb, which had turned up in 1903 and languished in a Vatican storeroom, was reattached (*right*).

A much more difficult task was posed by the discovery in the 1950s and 1960s of 20,000 fragments of other copies of Hellenistic originals by the same three men who carved the Laocoön. The pieces were recovered from a cave on Italy's Tyrrhenian coast that had served the first-century AD emperor Tiberius as a retreat. Matching these up and reassembling the statues fell to the classical scholar and sculptor Vittorio Moriello. From such fragments as a 10-foot-long leg, a giant hand, and two near-life-size torsos, Moriello was able to put together the reconstruction at right of the blinding of the Cyclops Polyphemus. He made fiberglass casts of the fragments and placed these where his knowledge of anatomy dictated that they should go. Moriello then filled the gaps with plaster, modeling it to conform to the figures' musculature.

Dwarfed by the reclining figure of the one-eyed Polyphemus, Vittorio Moriello climbs the Cyclops's body in a fiberglass and plaster restoration of an Odyssean sculpture group that adorned the emperor Tiberius's cave. The figure to the left of Moriello is thought to be Odysseus, who put out Polyphemus's eye.

Seen at near left is the Laocoön as it was reconstructed in the 16th century, with the priest's right arm raised and entwined with the serpents sent by the avenging sea god Poseidon. At far left is the same work, restored in 1960, with the extended arm replaced by the original. Since the earlier restoration required removing part of the shoulder, marble was added to the sculpture so the missing piece could be affixed at the proper angle. The figure on the right may not have been a part of the original Greek work, but added in the copy to reflect the Roman version of the story, which included a second son.

culture rather than the country itself. Scholars from Constantinople found ready employment as teachers of Greek in Venice, Florence, and Rome. The invention of printing provided a means for diffusing knowledge, and copies of the great works of Greece's golden age soon issued from the new presses.

In time, familiarity with Greek culture stimulated curiosity about Greece itself, and intrepid travelers made it their business to find out what survived of antiquity. None was more assiduous than Ciriaco Pizzicolli, known to history as Cyriac of Ancona after the port on Italy's Adriatic coast where he was born in 1391. A merchant, Cyriac traveled widely on trading trips. "I was pushed by an ardent desire to see the world," he wrote, "to seek out those monuments of antiquity scattered throughout the universe which have for so long been the principal object of my study."

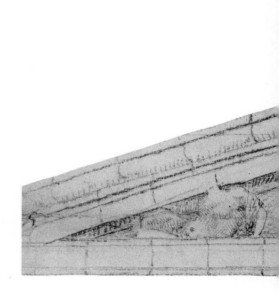

Pursuing the task tirelessly, Cyriac filled six notebooks with transcribed inscriptions and sketches of temples, monuments, and other artifacts. Fire, it is thought, consumed the books in 1514, leaving only one fragment in his own hand. But even this is enough for scholars to regard Cyriac—who saw the value of material remains when most humanists were collecting classical manuscripts—as the father of Greek archaeology.

Cyriac's last appearance in history is an ironic one. In 1453 the Ottoman Turks captured Constantinople, putting an end to the remnants of the thousand-year-old Byzantine Empire. A contemporary account pictures the ever-diplomatic Cyriac as reading from the Greek and Roman classics to Mehmed the Conqueror, the Ottoman sultan, on the eve of the final assault.

Unwittingly, Cyriac was assisting at the death of an era, for despite Mehmed's taste for classical learning, the triumph of the Turks again cut Greece off from the West. Soon after Constantinople had fallen, the Frankish possessions on mainland Greece also passed into Ottoman hands. Among the territories lost was Athens, where in 1460 the Muslim rulers added a minaret to the Parthenon, converting Athena's one-time temple into a mosque. Turkish attempts to expand their domain by wresting control of the Greek islands from the Venetians, however, led to persistent warfare between the two powers over the next two centuries.

The Turks triumphed, and for 150 years the conquered lands were off-limits to Westerners. Learning about conditions in Greece became so difficult that Martin Kraus, a professor at Tübingen dur-

Part of a series of drawings done by 17th-century French artist Jacques Carrey, this sketch of half of the Parthenon's western pediment offers a detailed view of the statuary before the temple was severely damaged in the Venetian siege of Athens in 1687 and subsequent Venetian attempts to remove them. The scene depicts a contest between Athena and Poseidon.

ing the mid-16th century, had to seek out correspondents in Constantinople and Greece to find out if Athens still existed.

The closing of Greece to the West did nothing, however, to diminish the enthusiasm for classical culture. The vogue for antique art reached new heights, and the wealthy and powerful vied to put together the finest collections. Before long every ruler on the Continent with any pretension to taste felt obliged to own an assortment of classical statuary. When originals became scarce, monarchs made do with copies instead.

In the 17th century, relations between the Ottoman Empire and the European powers thawed enough once more to permit occasional travel to Greece by Europeans. Most who ventured there, such as the Englishman William Petty, did so in search of art. Petty acquired more than 200 objects for the earl of Arundel (a famous connoisseur of Roman and Greek statuary) but only after losing a substantial number of marble works in a shipwreck and cooling his heels in prison for a spell while Turkish authorities tried to determine whether or not he was a spy.

An ambassador sent to the Levant to patch France's relations with the Ottomans, the marquis de Nointel, suffered no such setbacks. Thanks to his official status, he and an artist named Jacques Carrey were granted the privilege of touring Athens and the Acropolis in 1674. The timing of their visit was fortuitous, for only 13 years later, hostilities between the Ottoman Empire and Venice erupted again, and an artillery shell landed on the Parthenon, detonating ammunition the Turks had stored there and blowing sky-high many of Phidias's sculptures. Carrey's pencil studies are the only surviving visual record of what was lost.

In the same year that Carrey and Nointel visited the Parthenon, another Frenchman set out on a comprehensive tour that was to provide the material for the most detailed account of Greece's classical remains since Pausanias's day. Jacques Spon, the son of a Lyons doctor, spent the better part of a year roaming about Greece. He camped for days in parts of the countryside that were completely uninhabited and made do at times with nothing to eat but herbs and the hares that he and his English traveling companion could catch. Food, in fact, was a regular complaint. "One would suppose that to eat quantities of raw cucumber, even with sour milk, would be enough to kill a horse," Spon grumbled. "However, all those who have been in the Levant know that it is one of the greatest delicacies of the Turks." He was doubtlessly referring to a yogurt and cucumber soup or sauce still much eaten in Greece and Turkey today.

To his credit, Spon refused to let such matters of the stomach or the ever-present risk of being taken for a spy distract him from his task. In the course of his journey he copied more than 2,000 ancient inscriptions and used the information that they contained to identify many sites whose original Greek names had been lost. His narrative of his labors, entitled *The Journey to Italy, Dalmatia, Greece and the Levant*, was translated into several languages and became popular among the growing numbers of visitors who followed in his footsteps during the 18th century.

At that time, the influence of the intellectual movement known as the Enlightenment worked to lessen religious intolerance, and the rift between Christian Europe and the Muslims of the Ottoman Empire no longer excited such fierce ideological passions. This was also the era of the grand tour, when the sons of the wealthy were expected to travel to complete their education. Though their itineraries were normally limited to the social and artistic capitals of western Europe, the more adventurous among them took in the classical world of their studies.

In England, interest in Greece was further enhanced by the creation, in the 1730s, of the Society of Dilettanti, a small circle of well-to-do lovers of the arts. Scholars poked fun at the new organization, saying of its members that "the nominal qualification is having been in Italy, and the real one, being drunk," and for a time the carousing dilettantes did little to prove critics wrong. But in 1749 the gentlemen at last found a project worthy of their loftier passions: the production of a scholarly record of the ancient buildings of Athens by James Stuart, a painter, and Nicholas Revett, an architect.

Funded by the society, the pair spent almost two years studying—and tidying up—Athens. "We have carefully examined as low as to the foundation of every building that we have copied," they wrote in *The Antiquities of Athens,* the four-volume account they published of their work. "Tho' to perform this, it was generally necessary to get a great quantity of earth and rubbish removed; an operation which was sometimes attended with very considerable expense." Stuart and Revett even bought and demolished a house that obstructed their view of reliefs adorning the celebrated Tower of the Winds, a 40-foot-tall octagonal structure erected in the first century BC to hold a water clock. In place of the dwelling, they built another with a window specially positioned to give future travelers an unencumbered view of the carvings.

Although *The Antiquities of Athens* had a limited circulation, its influence was wide. From the time of the Renaissance, budding architects had been trained to emulate classical buildings, but these were largely based on Roman models. Now a vogue for Greek-inspired construction developed. Miniature versions of Greek temples—some designed by Stuart and Revett themselves on their return to England—sprang up in the gardens of great houses; churches and public edifices with columned porticoes modeled on the Parthenon adorned European cities. The newborn artistic movement was even to reach American shores: Greek revival architecture dotted the landscape of the Northeast with churches and houses that showed their debt to the past in their columns and pediments.

Neoclassicism, as the overall movement came to be known, took its theoretical underpinning from a German art historian whose work was contemporary with that of Stuart and Revett. But while the Englishmen studied the remains of ancient Greece, Johann Joachim Winckelmann was content to examine the Greek heritage in Rome and the newly rediscovered towns of Pompeii and Herculaneum. What he saw enabled him to assign individual Greek works, for the first time ever, to different periods and schools and convinced him that ancient Roman sculpture was at best an inspired copy and at worst a dull imitation of Greek originals. This view was to bring about a revolution in attitudes toward the two ancient cultures. "The only way for us to become great," Winckelmann wrote, "is to imitate the Greeks," and in so doing he gave neoclassicism its slogan.

Winckelmann's work, and that of Stuart, Revett, and their successors, kindled still greater enthusiasm for Greece and its culture as the 19th century dawned. But traveling conditions continued to be abominable, and questions remained about the land's historical geography. Three and a half centuries after the pioneering explorations of Cyriac of Ancona, many of the sites mentioned by the classical authors could no longer be identified with certainty.

Fortunately, William Martin Leake, a colonel in the British army, arrived in Greece in 1804, when Britain and France were at war with each other. Menaced by Napoleon, the Ottomans—whose empire was now in decline—turned to Britain for protection. Leake's mission was to confer with the local authorities to forestall a possible French attack on Greece. To keep him well occupied, he had been instructed to conduct a military assessment of the country and produce a study of its "general geography." Surveying tools in hand, Leake conscientiously explored mainland Greece off and on over the next five years, taking more than 1,500 measurements in the Peloponnese (then known as the Morea) alone. He also made himself something of a classical scholar, writing an eight-volume account of his labors, *Travels in Northern Greece and the Morea,* as well as separate volumes on the topography of Athens and its environs.

Leake's works made it easier than ever to find previously obscure classical sites. Travelers of every nationality, especially British, flooded the country: Artists of the budding romantic movement visited it in search of picturesque landscapes with ruins. Collectors arrived to buy ancient coins and vases and statues. Scholars came with Homer and Hesiod and Pindar in hand to enjoy the Greek poets in the land of their birth. Indeed, the very word *Greece* had become synonymous with artistic inspiration.

The country was to pay dearly for its new popularity, for the rivalries that drove the European powers to the battlefield also led to a fierce competition among them for ancient artworks. Each major country established a museum to stand as a symbol of its sophistication and then raced to acquire antiquities before they found their way into a competitor's collection. With the Greeks themselves still subjugated to the Ottomans and unable to protest, no monument of their ancient heritage was safe from the Germans, the French, the

English, and other Europeans who saw themselves as rescuing the past from years of neglect.

And so it was that Thomas Bruce, seventh earl of Elgin, the British envoy to the Ottoman court, became involved with the Athenian Parthenon, the very focal point of classical Greek civilization. It had been suggested to Elgin by the architect Thomas Harrison that casts of the Parthenon sculptures be made so that they might be brought back to Britain for educational purposes. With this aim in mind, Elgin approached various artists to supervise the molding, among them the great landscape and marine painter J. M. W. Turner, who wanted more money than Elgin could afford. Eventually, the job went to an Italian painter named Giovanni Battista Lusieri.

Dispatched to Athens with an international group of assistants while Elgin himself made his way to Constantinople to take up his official duties, Lusieri found the surviving statues in poor condition. Some had been defaced by the Ottoman garrison that occupied the Acropolis or pounded down as an ingredient for mortar. The Parthenon itself—still largely intact despite the 1687 explosion and known to the Turks as the "ancient temple of the idols"—had been raided for the lead in which the iron clamps used to hold the blocks of the columns together had been set. "I am sure," he wrote to Elgin, "that in half a century there will not remain one stone on another."

Convinced as he was that he was helping to preserve a vital part of the human heritage, Elgin used his influence at the Ottoman court to obtain a letter called a firman that permitted his agents not merely to copy the works but also to "take away any pieces of stone with old inscriptions or figures thereon." Whether this phrase, taken from an ambiguously worded Italian translation of the Turkish original—which has long since vanished—authorized the events that followed has been the subject of bitter controversy for more than a century. What is known is that the Turkish grand vizier in Athens raised no objections to the liberal interpretation of the firman's wording favored by Elgin's chaplain, Philip Hunt, who was sent to supervise the work. Presented with gifts of cut glass and firearms,

Striking a casual pose, a young Lord Elgin exudes the confidence that enabled him to lay claim to some of Greece's greatest treasures, sculptures from the Parthenon and other structures on the Acropolis, and ship them home to England. An ulceration, probably brought on by mercury treatments for syphilis, would eventually eat away much of his nose and leave him pitifully disfigured.

19

the vizier looked the other way while Hunt's team set about the removal of numerous Parthenon sculptures.

In contrast, Edward Dodwell, an English traveler, watched with "inexpressible mortification" as the workers loosened the reliefs called metopes and triglyphs. "I saw several metopae in the south east extremity of the temple taken down," the Englishman wrote. "They were fixed in between the triglyphs as in a groove; and in order to lift them up, it was necessary to throw to the ground the magnificent cornice by which they were covered. The south east angle of the pediment shared the same fate."

Hunt's men freed 56 sections of the friezes and pried loose a dozen or so statues from the two pediments. They also took the scattered bas-reliefs and friezes of the small temple of Athena Nike, which had graced the entrance to the Acropolis until 1687, when it was dismantled to make way for a Turkish bastion. They even removed one of the six sculpted female figures, or caryatids, that supported the roof of the south porch of the Erechtheum (the asymmetrical, four-chambered shrine located north of the Parthenon), replacing the maiden with an unsightly brick pillar.

Twenty-two ships were required to carry the marbles to Britain. One was wrecked en route; recovering its cargo took three years. Elgin himself had an equally eventful journey. Taking advantage of a cessation of hostilities in the Napoleonic Wars to return home through France, he was unable to proceed when the truce abruptly ended and was obliged to remain there for three years as an enemy national while his treasures sat in storage.

When he finally reached London, Elgin at once made arrangements to display the marbles, hiring a prizefighter to pose alongside them to illustrate a theory that "the science of sculptors cannot so effectually be promoted, as by athletic exercises practised in the presence of similar works." But public reaction was not unanimously favorable. One critic, an influential member of the Society of Dilettanti, belittled the statues as mere Roman copies. "You have lost your labors, my Lord Elgin," he wrote. "Your marbles are overrated. They are not Greek. They are Roman of the time of Hadrian."

Artists were more discerning. The great Italian sculptor Antonio Canova, whom Elgin had invited to restore those of the statues that were damaged, refused on the grounds that it would be sacrilege to touch them. Even more remarkable was the response of the English painter Benjamin Robert Haydon, a friend of the poet John

In this 1818 painting, items taken from the Acropolis in Athens by Lord Elgin—metopes from the Parthenon (top) and a caryatid from the Erechtheum (far right)—are displayed with the frieze from the Temple of Apollo at Bassae discovered by Xeneion member Charles Cockerell. The artist glamorized the temporary setting in which the British Museum displayed these recently acquired works.

Keats. "I drew at the marbles ten, fourteen, and fifteen hours at a time; staying often till twelve at night, holding a candle and my board in one hand and drawing with the other," Haydon wrote in his journals. "Oh, those days of luxury and rapture and uncontaminated purity of mind! I arose with the sun and opened my eyes to its light only to be conscious of my high pursuit; I sprang from my bed, dressed as if possessed, and passed the day, the noon and the night in the same dream of abstracted enthusiasm."

Some within the artistic community expressed their dismay over the means Elgin had used to obtain the marbles. The poet Lord

Byron, who would hurry to Greece in the 1820s along with a thousand other Europeans to join that country's successful eight-year fight for independence, thundered against the "dull spoiler" who had carried off the "last poor plunder from a bleeding land" and compared the earl unfavorably to Alaric the Visigoth, conqueror of Rome, who at least had won his booty in battle.

Alarmed by such criticism, the British government, to whom Elgin had always intended to sell the marbles, initially refused to meet the price he asked. Several years passed before Parliament finally came up with an offer of £35,000, which Elgin accepted unenthusiastically. He claimed that obtaining the marbles had cost him £72,000, inclusive of interest on the capital expended. The sculptures were moved to the British Museum in London, where despite Greek demands for their return, they remain to this day. The museum argues that to return them would set a precedent that could empty museums around the world.

One reason for the English government's change of heart was the favorable reception that was given to another frieze that arrived in Britain in the interim. This one came from the Temple of Apollo at Bassae, a remote and little-visited site about 20 miles southeast of Olympia in the Peloponnese. The work had been found by the Xeneion, the first international group of architects and writers to dedicate themselves to the recovery of Greek antiquities. Comprising Germans, Englishmen, and Danes, the circle had only one membership requirement—that its fellows share an "enthusiasm for Greece, ancient literature, and the fine arts."

With the Xeneion, the age of Greek archaeology can properly be said to have got under way, for they were among the first explorers to excavate sites in search of buried finds. Earlier visitors had on the whole avoided digging, partly because there was so much to be discovered above ground but also because it attracted the suspicions of local people, who assumed buried treasure lay at hand.

Xeneion members used charm and sheer force of numbers to avoid any such problems at Bassae and also on Aegina, an island lying southwest of Athens in the Saronic Gulf, where in April 1811 they excavated the ruins of the Temple of Aphaia, a fertility goddess related to Artemis. As described by one participant, the English architect Charles Cockerell, the atmosphere of the digs—except for the danger of pirates lurking offshore—was pastoral: "We got our provisions and labourers from the town, our fuel was the wild thyme, there were abundance of partridges to eat, and we bought kids from the shepherds; and when work was over for the day, there was grand roasting of them over a blazing fire with an accompaniment of native music, singing and dancing."

Both ventures met with outstanding success. "On the second day," Cockerell wrote of the Aegina discoveries, "one of the excavators, working in the interior portico, struck on a piece of Parian marble which, as the building itself is of stone, arrested his attention. It turned out to be the head of a helmeted warrior, perfect in every feature. It lay with the face turned upwards, and as the features came out by degrees you can imagine nothing like the state of rapture and excitement to which we were wrought. Here was an altogether new interest, which set us to work with a will."

Soon another head was turned up, Cockerell reports, then a leg and a foot, until "no less than sixteen statues and thirteen heads, legs, arms, etc." were finally found under the fallen portions of the eastern and western pediments. Once officials of the island were amply compensated, the marbles were spirited "without delay" to Piraeus, Athens's seaport, and carried from there to the capital at night "to avoid exciting attention."

Equally good fortune awaited Cockerell at Bassae. Poking in late summer through the rubble that covered the site, the architect noticed a fox bolting from a hole under a mass of stone. Examining the animal's den, he found himself gazing upon a bas-relief that turned out to be part of a 101-foot-long continuous frieze depicting, among other things, the victory of the Lapiths, a legendary people said to have descended from Apollo, over the half-horse, half-human centaurs. To fifth-century BC Greeks, this encounter symbolized civilization's triumph over barbarity.

Though beautiful, the sculptures failed to impress the Turkish governor of the Peloponnese, who was hoping for items of silver or gold to take to market. He sold his half interest in the excavation to the Xeneion for £400. The frieze was eventually auctioned to Britain's prince regent for considerably more—£15,000 (about $606,000 in today's currency). The Aegina statues went to King Ludwig I of Bavaria for a smaller but still substantial amount.

Thanks to the largesse of such collectors, the passion for Greek treasure hunting soon reached fever pitch. Following in the

Probably the world's most famous statue, the Venus de Milo stands boxed in, during an 1871 restoration. The second-century BC work was found in two large pieces and several smaller fragments by a farmer on the Greek island of Melos in 1820. Recognizing the sculpture's importance, a Frenchman who was present at the time offered to buy it, but all his subsequent efforts were thwarted and the Venus seemed about to pass into the hands of a Greek dignitary. Only aggressive, last-minute negotiations, aided by the presence of a French warship, ensured that it went to France.

steps of Jacques Spon and others, adventurous explorers widened the scope of their searches to include the wealthy and cultivated kingdoms that flourished long ago on the Turkish side of the Aegean but now slumbered in what one scholar termed "reedy desolation." Among these sites was Halicarnassus, a little town on the Aegean coast dominated by an imposing castle built in the 15th century by the crusading Knights of St. John.

Now the city of Bodrum, Halicarnassus in the fourth century BC was the seat of power of Mausolus, ruler of the kingdom of Caria and satrap for the king of Persia. After his death in 353 BC, Mausolus was laid to rest in a gleaming tomb said to be so massive it was visible from ships at sea and so lavishly decorated it too became known as one of the Seven Wonders of the World. According to the Roman naturalist Pliny the Elder, the monument—called the Mausoleum after its powerful owner—had three layers, each of which was decorated with statuary. A lofty, rectangular podium formed the foundation. On it sat a colonnade of 36 columns and a stepped, pyramidal roof topped with a marble statue of a four-horse chariot.

The Mausoleum was still intact in the 13th century; sometime thereafter it collapsed for reasons unknown. In 1494, when the knights decided to refortify their castle, they had no farther to look than the ruins of the great tomb itself for building materials. By 1522 almost nothing remained to be seen. Many of the Mausoleum's marble statues had been smashed and burned to make lime mortar, while some of its reliefs had been incorporated into the castle walls for decoration. The green volcanic stone from its core had been fashioned into ramparts, and the tomb chamber had been looted.

The castle subsequently fell to the Turks and for many years most Westerners were denied access to it. One French antiquarian obtained a firman permitting him to enter but declined to use it when the fortress commander pointed out that the document said nothing about the Frenchman's ever coming out again.

Later explorers, including an 18th-century English traveler named Richard Dalton, had better luck. Dalton not only gained admission to the castle but published several drawings of surviving portions of a frieze depicting a battle between Greeks and Amazons, as well as sketches of other pieces. A century later the reliefs attracted the attention of Viscount Stratford de Redcliffe, British envoy to Constantinople, who in 1846 obtained permission to remove what was left of the Amazon frieze.

Presented to the British Museum as gifts from the sultan, the sculptures excited the curiosity of Charles Newton, the assistant curator. Newton, a tall, strong man with a thick, dark beard that gave him the look of a "weather-worn antique Zeus," determined to devote all his considerable energies to finding and reconstructing the Mausoleum. Although no visible sign of the tomb survived where it had stood, Newton identified the location in Bodrum from a description written in the first century BC by the Roman architect and engineer Vitruvius. Unfortunately, houses covered much of the site. Before he could start digging, Newton had to buy these up, and much time was spent haggling over questions of financial compensation. When work finally got under way in early 1857, Newton uncovered hundreds of sculpture fragments but came away disappointed. The majority of the marbles, he wrote, "had evidently been rolled and pitched out of the way by the spoilers of the tomb," making it impossible to specify where on the Mausoleum the pieces originally had been located. His efforts, it seemed, were in vain.

But then Charles Newton's luck changed. Opting to dig into a rising slope that provided deeper soil cover than the rest of the site, he discovered a major deposit of sculptures. In an area about 60 feet long and 20 feet wide, he found 66 statues or fragments of statuary, including substantial sections of horses from the chariot group that had crowned the monument; several stone lions resembling those preserved in the castle, only in better condition; and a pair of colossal portrait figures that Newton identified, perhaps optimistically, as Mausolus and his wife, Artemisia.

The pieces, which duly found their way to the British Museum, had survived only because the collapse of the building had thrown them outside a wall that surrounded the Mausoleum and into an area the Knights of St. John would leave undisturbed. Their loss was archaeology's gain, for the sculptures enabled Newton to make

All that remains on the site of the Mausoleum are these ruins, investigated in recent times by Danish archaeologist Kristian Jeppesen and his team. In the left foreground lies the large stone that blocked the funeral chamber. In spite of this impediment, graverobbers entered the tomb and plundered it, leaving only a few gold spangles in the dust. Just in front of the stone, Jeppesen found a buried offering consisting of butchered calves, sheep, oxen, chickens, doves, and a goose.

assumptions about the tomb's colonnade and roof that ultimately laid the groundwork for modern reconstructions of the Mausoleum and helped to fulfill, at least in small part, Mausolus's ambition to be remembered for all time.

In the following decade, Newton was to play a part in the investigation of yet another wonder of the ancient world—the enormous Temple of Artemis at Ephesus, a city near the Aegean coast, about 60 miles north of Halicarnassus. Begun in the sixth century BC by Croesus, the legendary wealthy ruler of Lydia, the shrine served as a destination for countless pilgrims until destroyed in the third century AD by rampaging Goths. Then a nearby river flooded, covering the ruins and the city port with silt, and Ephesus disappeared. By the 19th century, no trace could be found of the fabled temple, the home of the "Diana of the Ephesians" mentioned in the Bible (Diana being the Roman name of the goddess Artemis). Newton persuaded the British Museum to back an attempt to find it.

The man who set out to locate it was John Turtle Wood, an English engineer working on the construction of railway lines in Turkey and a newcomer to archaeology. Like Newton at Halicarnassus, Wood had found clues to work from in the writings of Vitruvius, Strabo, Pliny, Pausanias, Herodotus, and other ancient authors. They indicated that the temple was located outside the city walls and that a road led to it from the so-called Magnesian Gate. A 600-foot-long stoa, or colonnaded walk, built by a wealthy Roman donor stood beside the route, which passed the tomb of Androclus, the legendary founder of Ephesus.

Wood started work in the spring of 1863. As the silting that had blocked the port had also turned much of the site into a marsh, it took him more than four years just to trace the remains of the Magnesian Gate. He then started excavating the road that led from it, only to find that it divided soon after. He was forced to explore both of the forks until, 500 yards down one of them, he came upon traces of a Roman stoa.

Wood knew now that he was on the right track, but his problems continued to multiply. He was plagued by bouts of malaria and pressed for funds. (He had already broken his collarbone when his horse fell in a ditch, and he had been knifed by a madman who mistook him for the local British consul, against whom the Turk had a grudge.) But the British Museum—probably at Newton's behest—came to Wood's aid and provided a further grant.

FRAGMENTS OF A LOST WONDER

Gone but hardly forgotten, the Hellenistic Mausoleum at Halicarnassus (today's Bodrum, in Turkey), one of the Seven Wonders of the World, long teased with the scant remains of its glory. What had it looked like to have deserved such an epithet?

Descriptions by classical authors provided a partial picture, and several artists' reconstructions were attempted. But not until in-depth studies of information collected at the site during 19th- and 20th-century excavations and a careful examination of the surviving fragments could the monument's true splendor be recaptured—on paper. One such modern reconstruction by British archaeologist Geoffrey Waywell, used here as a background, suggests how the sculptures might have been arranged on the multitiered building. Ancient writers gave the Mausoleum's height variously, ranging from 140 feet to 180 feet; Waywell went with 140 feet.

Faced with white marble and blue limestone, the Mausoleum must have bedazzled viewers—and all the more so because its sculptures and architectural details were brightly painted. Pieces excavated in the 1850s and in more recent times have revealed a range of colors: red, blue, purple, brown, and yellow.

This portion of a giant horse, which likely measured 12 feet high and 14 feet long, belonged to the team of four drawing a chariot that once topped the Mausoleum. Any accompanying figures probably would have stood over 16 feet tall. Hoisting the group into position posed a great challenge to the monument's builders.

Best preserved of the figures that may have graced the columned upper tier, this male and female pair were dubbed Mausolus and Artemisia by their discoverer in 1857, though current thinking does not identify them as the husband and wife builders of the monument, but rather as two of their ancestors coming to pay homage.

The next year Wood found vestiges of Androclus's tomb but again ran into difficulties when the road he was excavating crossed into fields of ripe barley. Harvest time was approaching, and he could not afford to buy up the growing crop. So work again came to a halt while the farmers brought in the grain. By the time they had finished, the firman authorizing the work had run out.

At this moment of despair, Wood's fortunes improved. Almost at once after having the permit renewed, he uncovered remnants of a massive stone wall—a find that secured him one more grant from the museum. Then, recommencing the excavation, he quickly turned up two large inscriptions, one in Latin, the other in Greek. These declared that the wall had been built by the Roman emperor Augustus in the year 6 BC to enclose the Temple of Artemis. Wood had reached his goal.

In 1869 the British Museum bought the entire site, and Wood set to work excavating the temple itself. He unearthed a mosaic pavement first, then six fluted column drums and a column base and capital, an extraordinary discovery that drew a number of notable visitors to Ephesus. Among them was the German businessman turned archaeologist Heinrich Schliemann, who arrived in December of 1870. Schliemann had just finished his first season of excavations at Troy, located 150 miles northwest of Ephesus, and would soon uncover remains of the city, scene of the epic siege that is described in Homer's *Iliad*. Schliemann, Wood noted, was "kindly enthusiastic in his congratulations."

In the course of three more years' work, Wood and his team cleared more than 132,000 cubic yards of earth and shipped to the British Museum in the spring of 1873 alone more than 60 tons of architectural and sculptural remains. One of the pieces they sent—a huge section of a frieze showing Greeks and Amazons—weighed no less than 11 tons. When workers at first tried to move it from the site, the road cracked and gave way.

The size of the haul alone could not atone for the archaeological sins Wood committed while searching for the temple. He rarely obtained permission to dig from landowners, for instance, and

Houses still cling to the slopes of Mount Parnassus in this photograph, taken in the 1890s as excavation of the sacred site of Delphi encroaches on the village of Kastri. The exposed ruins of the Temple of Apollo's northeastern terrace are visible in the foreground. Some 1,000 structures had to be bought and torn down to make way for the archaeologists.

Marking the moment of a major find on May 30, 1894, excavators at Delphi cluster around the upper portion of an archaic-period kouros, or a standing nude male, that they have just extracted from a modern masonry wall.

sank holes unsystematically and recklessly, with tragic results. One of his trenches caved in because its sides were not shored up adequately, and the hired hand who was working in it lost his life. Wood also failed to publish an account of the excavation that was detailed enough for future researchers to trace his steps.

Fortunately, archaeology in Greece itself was soon to be put on new, and sounder, footing by a German team that in 1875 had begun a thorough investigation of Olympia. Over six seasons, the

Germans uncovered the entire sacred precinct surrounding the Temple of Zeus, laying the groundwork for the discovery of Phidias's workshop some 80 years later, and turned up hundreds of inscriptions, terra cottas, bronze objects, and marble sculptures. Among these was a statue of the youthful god Hermes cradling his infant brother Dionysus that is thought to be a copy of a work by the great fourth-century BC sculptor Praxiteles.

No matter how much the Germans might covet the beautiful statues, they could not remove the pieces, nor could they take any of the other finds home with them, for their campaign was the subject of a legally binding agreement—the first such ever between sovereign states. Signed in April 1874 and known as the Olympia Convention, the pact gave the Germans the rights to control every aspect of the work under Greek supervision and to make copies and casts of all finds so long as they paid the expenses of the excavation and all the originals remained in Greece.

The excavation that followed established new standards of accuracy and attention to detail. Aiming to unearth the ground plan and history not just of a single building but of an entire monumental complex, the Germans kept a daily journal of their work and made a careful inventory of the exact circumstances of each find. Artists made drawings of the sculptures upon discovery, often before they had been fully unearthed. And unlike Wood, the archaeologists wrote up detailed reports of the excavation that were published at regular intervals, to bring the findings to the attention of the wider world.

This new, respectful approach set a pattern that was followed wholeheartedly in the years to come by the schools of archaeology the Western powers were founding at the time in Athens. The French had established the first such school as early as 1846, 9 years after the formation of the Greek Archaeological Society and just 17 years after the Greeks emancipated themselves from Turkish rule. Now the Germans, Americans, and British followed suit, and the Austrians and Italians joined them in the ensuing decades.

Yet excavation remained a tricky and expensive business, as the French learned when they negotiated to explore Delphi, about 80 miles northwest of Athens, home of Greece's most famous oracle. In ancient times, postulants came to its Temple of Apollo, perched dramatically beneath 800-foot cliffs on the slopes of Mount Parnassus, to seek advice on important matters. After bathing in the waters of a nearby spring, the pilgrims would sacrifice a goat, sheep, or ox to the god before entering the temple.

Inside, they were directed to a stone sanctuary from which a staircase descended into a subterranean vault. There the priestess of the oracle, an untutored local woman, sat suspended over a fissure in the rock from which foul-smelling gases issued, apparently emerging from the very bowels of the earth. Inspired as it seemed by the god himself, the priestess uttered her response, which the priests of the temple subsequently translated into pithy rhymes.

The advice the oracle offered was often notoriously ambiguous in nature. For example, when Philip II, king of Macedon in the fourth century BC, asked whether he should invade Persia, he was informed, "The bull is garlanded. All is done. The sacrificer is ready." Assuming that the priestess was predicting the demise of the Persian emperor, Philip planned his attack—but was struck down by an assassin before it could begin.

The site of the temple was obviously a tempting target for archaeologists, and the Greek government determined to wrest the maximum possible advantage from the foreigners' interest. In return for the right to excavate, the French were asked to reduce import duties on the raisins for which the Greek town of Corinth was well known. Regarding this as an attempt at commercial blackmail, the French refused, only to see the coveted site offered to Germany

Onlookers crowd onto the site where the bronze Charioteer of Delphi (right) was discovered in 1896. Excited by the find, the spectators trampled and all but obliterated the historical context in which the statue lay, making it impossible to find out just when the figure was toppled and buried.

instead. When these negotiations also failed, the French finally managed to negotiate suitable terms—and then learned that the inhabitants of Kastri, the village that had grown up on top of Delphi, violently opposed the excavation, which required them to give up their houses and move to a new community nearby. Resettling the townsfolk took several years, and resentments lingered. When the French finally began clearing the site in 1892, they had to do so under armed guard.

In archaeological terms, Delphi's treasures have proved to be worth the wait. The excavations, which still continue, have yielded remains of some 235 buildings and monuments. In addition, the on-site museum now contains more than 7,000 objects. Perhaps the most prized of these is a magnificent bronze almost six feet tall known as the Charioteer of Delphi, which was discovered in pieces in late April and early May of 1896.

The lower half of the statue appeared first, while workers led by Théophile Homolle, director of the French School of Archaeology at Athens, were dismantling an old water conduit on the site of a demolished house. The figure, recalled the excavators, was barefoot but clad in an ankle-length tunic whose folds fell "with the regularity of Ionic column fluting." A right forearm and hand, three fragments of reins still clutched in its fingers, turned up three days later, along with the charioteer's upper torso and head.

The figure was part of a large bronze group that included a

31

chariot and four horses. An inscribed block, bearing a dedication in verse, found at the same time states that Polyzalos, the ruler of Gela, an old Greek colony on Sicily, commissioned the work to celebrate his victory in races run at Delphi during the Pythian Games of 478 or 474 BC. On view today at the Delphi Museum, the Charioteer stands as one of the world's most prized artworks. Upon viewing his young, confident face, wrote a Greek archaeologist, "the spectator is carried back in time to that triumphant moment when the victorious charioteer, proud and self-controlled at the same time, receives the crowd's applause as if it were an additional laurel wreath."

The statue's discovery typifies the approach of modern archaeologists, who as a rule seek not to enhance the glory of some noble patron or the collections of a great museum but to pursue knowledge of ancient Greece for its own sake. In this regard, Delphi has proved to be a mine of historical information, as excavators have unearthed dozens of inscriptions put up by the individual city-states that then made up Greece to commemorate victories in battles and sporting events such as the Pythian Games.

But Delphi has also helped to shed light on Greek prehistory—the little-studied centuries in which the developments of the classical age were incubating—for here excavators have unearthed evidence of a settlement that existed more than 3,300 years ago until destroyed at the end of the Mycenaean era. Its last residents had been dead for centuries when Apollo's cult took root in the area. Discovering what life was like after their demise, and before the first pilgrims made their way from the city-states, represents perhaps the biggest challenge for classical archaeologists today. ⊠

IMAGES OF AN AWAKENED PAST

One moonlit summer night in 1867, an adventurous American traveler secretly slipped ashore from his quarantined ship in the harbor of Piraeus. Dodging police patrols, he hiked the six and a half miles into Athens, then gained access to the Acropolis by bribing some of the guards. Utterly captivated by the moon-washed ruins, he marveled at the scene around him: "Set up in rows—stacked up in piles—scattered broadcast over the wide area of the Acropolis—were hundreds of crippled statues of all sizes and of the most exquisite workmanship." This nighttime intruder was none other than the American author Mark Twain, who recounted his escapade in the book *The Innocents Abroad*.

Twain's reverent pilgrimage typifies the mid-19th century's fascination with all things Greek and also points up the dichotomy of the Victorian era. Technological advances (such as the steamship that had carried Twain to Europe) were pulling the world into a new,

industrial age at breakneck pace, but many poets, writers, and philosophers of the time chose to dwell in the past, drawing their inspiration from the Greek world.

Quite naturally, scholarly attention—including the nascent science of archaeology—focused on Greece, only recently liberated from nearly four centuries of Turkish rule. Additionally, one of the 19th century's most auspicious inventions, the camera, could now provide academicians and armchair travelers alike with true-to-life images of exotic, faraway places.

Pioneering photographers such as the American William J. Stillman—using bulky cameras with fragile glass-plate negatives—bequeathed an invaluable record of archaeological sites, such as the Acropolis, the focus of this picture essay. But Stillman, in particular, composed his views with an artistic eye as well. His shot of a tumbled, broken relief from the balustrade of the Temple of Athena Nike *(above)* provides a haunting visual counterpart to Twain's stirring prose.

This 1865 photo depicts an early phase in archaeological exploration of the Acropolis. Most of these statues were desecrated in 480 BC by the Persians, then buried by the Athenians. Among them are the now famed *Calf Bearer* and the *Kritios Boy* (on the right).

Stillman's atmospheric 1869 portrait of the Parthenon shows the Acropolis partially cleared of the Turkish buildings that hemmed in the ancient monuments on the summit. Renovation of the temples and systematic excavation of the grounds have not yet begun.

Victorian tourists take in the sights around the ruined shell of the Erechtheum in 1859. Ironically, some of the greatest damage to the 2,300-year-old temple had occurred a mere three decades earlier, during the Greek War of Independence, when Turkish gunpowder that was stored in the northern porch (left) exploded.

Two photos from the 1860s reflect the formidable challenge early archaeologists faced in discerning order among the jumbled debris and postclassical structures strewn about the Acropolis. Excavated sculpted heads (above), temporarily stockpiled at the top of the Propylaea stairs, seem to be searching for their long-lost bodies. The foundation of the small Ionic Temple of Athena Nike at the upper-right corner of the Propylaea (right) had only been exposed in 1835 when a Turkish gun bastion was removed. The medieval square tower behind the temple would be razed in 1875 as part of an ongoing effort to restore the site as much as possible to its ancient appearance.

This 1865 photograph of the Acropolis clearly shows several large rubble dumps below the summit that resulted from the demolition of the hill's Turkish structures. The Propylaea and the still-intact medieval tower are at left.

SHINING NEW LIGHT ON GREECE'S DARK AGE

During the summer, birds of prey wheel in lazy circles about the sheer cliffs that rise 3,000 feet above Chalcis, on the large Aegean island of Euboea. Separated from the Greek mainland by the 43-yard width of the Euripos Channel, the island is reached by a bridge. Beside this bridge tourists watch, fascinated, as the current changes direction from north-south to south-north and back, a phenomenon occurring at least six times a day. But the place has something else to excite imaginations. Just to the south in the Bay of Aulis, according to Homer, the Greek ships assembled before setting sail for Troy; here King Agamemnon of Mycenae allegedly sacrificed his daughter Iphigenia in the hope of gaining a favorable wind.

It is only fitting, therefore, that an island as redolent of ancient Greek history as Euboea should have opened to archaeologists a new vista on a puzzling era. The dramatic shift occurred in 1981 with the investigation of a hillock, Toumba, not far from the village of Lefkandi. Preliminary excavations by the British School of Archaeology in Athens in the 1960s had revealed a cemetery, but it would be more than a decade before the mound yielded its most fascinating secrets.

The circumstances were strange: The summit of Toumba belonged to a local Greek, who in 1980 applied for permission to build on the site. The application was referred to the Greek Archae-

Unearthed near the village of Lefkandi, on the Greek island of Euboea, this terracotta centaur dates from the 10th century BC but shows influences of the much earlier civilization of the Mycenaeans.

ological Service, which then carried out trial excavations to assess the site's archaeological value. These digs revealed the stone foundations of a large building with substantial walls dating from the 10th century BC, and plans were made for a major excavation.

Before the dig could begin, however, the owner decided to take matters into his own hands and strike when least expected. On the day of the Feast of the Panayia in August 1980—a holy day celebrated by all Greeks, including the members of the Greek Archaeological Service—a bulldozer came chugging up Toumba Hill. Upon reaching the summit, it proceeded to level the building site down to a depth of nearly 10 feet. The bulldozer pursued its task until it had destroyed one-third of the ancient building so recently identified by the archaeologists. Rushing in to save what was left, a collaboration of the Greek Archaeological Service, represented by Eva Touloupa, and the British School of Archaeology in Athens, under the Oxford University archaeologist Mervyn Popham, scheduled a full-scale excavation on Toumba the following spring.

As the excavation of 1981 unfolded, the archaeologists knew, based on previous digs, that they were exploring not only an immense building but also an area that was part of a large, prosperous community. That community had continued functioning from the early Bronze Age to around 700 BC, through a depressed period traditionally designated as the Greek dark age.

Particularly revealing were five cemeteries, one of which proved rich in grave goods. The provenance of some of the objects astonished the team. The Euboeans supposedly were a backward, isolated people—yet one grave contained vases from Attica on the Greek mainland, bronze wheels from Cyprus, and a ring with a cut gem depicting Amen, the ram-headed god of Egypt. More surprising was the discovery of two Egyptian bronze vases in two other graves, suggesting that the Euboeans of the 10th century BC had trading contact with Egypt.

In the millennium and a half before the Toumba burials, three magnificent Bronze Age civilizations had flourished in the sea-girt realm that would become the Greece of the classical era. The Cycladic culture developed on the circle of Aegean islands southeast of the mainland, early in the Bronze Age, between 3500 and 2000 BC, and was followed by the Minoan civilization (2000 to 1470 BC), centered on the island of Crete. The Minoans created brilliant art and a gracious way of life, which offered civic amenities not seen again in

This skeleton—possibly the remains of a woman sacrificed at the burial of her warrior-husband—was discovered in a tomb near Lefkandi. The body was adorned with a delicate gold pendant and necklace, gilt hair ornaments, and the striking pair of gold breastplates seen resting on her chest.

Europe for a thousand years. Among the features that characterized this culture was its writing, known as Linear A and still untranslated.

Even as the Minoans were reaching their apex, another late Bronze Age culture was developing on the mainland in centers such as Athens, Tiryns, Pylos, and Mycenae, which gave this civilization its name—Mycenaean. The Mycenaeans borrowed much from the Minoans, whom they superseded, while developing their own life-style. That they were a Greek-speaking people became known when their written language, called Linear B, was deciphered in 1952.

Both the Mycenaeans and the earlier Minoans lived in what archaeologists called palace cultures, societies that revolved around great stone-palace complexes whose inhabitants, believed to be hereditary kings and their administrators, made and enforced laws and governed the economy. The Mycenaeans built upon high bluffs their fortresslike palaces known as acropolises, Greek for "top cities."

After growing ever more powerful, the Mycenaeans suffered a cataclysmic collapse between 1250 and 1190 BC, probably brought about by a combination of events. Archaeologists have suggested possible causes—civil war, revolution, and invasion among them. These most likely combined with some widespread economic hardship such as famine. Whatever the reasons, the Mycenaean palace system of government disappeared, most of the great palace centers were destroyed or abandoned, and many of the survivors fled to the outer fringes of the Greek world—the coastal regions and the islands. The Mycenaeans vanished as an identifiable people, and a dark age descended over the Greek world that would last for some 300 years. Into the vacuum moved simpler folk, the mysterious Dorians of legend, believed by many scholars to have been Greek-speaking tribes that migrated from the mountainous, barbarous north.

Little is known about this period, hence its name the dark age. The Linear B script, used exclusively by palace scribes, had disappeared with the collapse of the palace system. Representative art declined, leaving scant pictorial evidence behind to fill in the gaps in the archaeological record. Scholars have strained to provide a meager portrait: Pottery yields throughout Greece and the islands suggest a massive population decline over a period of time, as does a 1964 survey of habitation sites showing 320 locations occupied in the 13th century BC, 130 in the 12th, and 40 in the 11th. By 1000 BC four-fifths of the Mycenaean sites had been abandoned, with many regions and islands totally depopulated. For the century following the Mycenaean collapse, archaeologists have found no Greek artifact on any site overseas and no foreign artifact on Greek soil.

Widespread poverty is evidenced by an absence, scarcity, or downgrading of the simpler material objects of life. Arrowheads made of obsidian instead of metal appear in graves throughout the Greek mainland. Rings of bone, beads of clay, slingshots of stone instead of lead, all betoken personal and communal penury and a lack of materials. And Greece suffered a severe shortage of such commonplace everyday items as lamps, suggesting that the dark age may have been dark indeed.

From this benighted wasteland another Greek world slowly emerged, forging a new culture that spawned art, philosophy, and literature. It eventually spread around much of the Mediterranean littoral, to become the heritage of the entire Western world. From the 11th century BC onward, the Greeks experienced successive periods of development, which scholars have named for the pottery characteristic of each era. Roughly, the so-called protogeometric style lasted from 1050 to 900 BC; the geometric, between 900 and 750 BC; and the orientalizing, 750 to 600 BC.

As they rose to new heights of economic and artistic output, the Greeks would travel over land and sea, trading and colonizing wherever they went, absorbing into their own way of life whatever

CHANGING STYLES IN VASE PAINTING

The ancient Greeks seldom inscribed clear dates at sites that would one day be plumbed by archaeologists. But they did leave behind clues. Chief among them, perhaps, are various styles of vase painting, which evolved in such a definite progression that a knowledgeable researcher can determine a site's time period with fair precision simply by examining the sherds found there.

Representative vases from four major periods are shown below. The earliest style seen here, known as geometric, flourished from the 10th to the eighth century BC and relied on straight lines and repetitions of basic shapes, such as circles, squares, and triangles.

Toward the end of the eighth century animal forms began to

GEOMETRIC   ORIENTALIZING   BLACK-FIGURE

appear and rapidly supplanted geometric patterns as the preferred decoration on Greek vases. Because some of the animals were exotic beasts from the East, the stylistic era is known as the orientalizing period.

After about a century, animal motifs started giving way to representations of humans done in the black-figure technique—so called because the subjects were rendered as black silhouettes, which were then detailed with a sharp instrument and with colors. A foremost black-figure artist was the sixth-century Athenian painter Exekias, whose depiction of Achilles and Ajax playing at dice appears here.

As the sixth century drew to a close, yet another style of vase painting, known as red-figure, came to the fore. Working in this mode, artists made their backgrounds black and left their figures the natural red color of the clay, as in the portrayal of the goddess Nike shown below.

RED-FIGURE

pleased them in other cultures, in the process transforming the acquired trait into something peculiarly Greek. These traders and colonists would take with them overseas crucial elements of their motherland—their way of organizing the fundamental political unit of their culture, the city-state, as well as their language, gods, literature, philosophy, and science. In time they would turn the Mediterranean Sea into a Greek lake. By the fifth century, the philosopher Plato could say the Greeks had become like "ants or frogs round a pond."

Even during the long, bleak interregnum between the end of the Mycenaeans and the rise of a new Greek civilization, there were signs of a change for the better in the quality of Greek life. A major technological advance—the replacement of bronze with iron—broadly coincided with the onset of the dark age. Iron gradually became the principal metal in the Greek world, especially for making weapons. And there were pockets of survival. Athens held out against the general ruin from the outset. Some of the large Aegean islands also seemed to thrive.

The discovery at Lefkandi certainly indicated that Euboea was prosperous in this early period. The building partially destroyed by the bulldozer turned out to be the largest and most sophisticated structure of the era so far uncovered, measuring at least 135 feet in length and 30 feet in width. In its central room the archaeologists found a rock-hewn shaft containing two compartments. In one lay the skeletons of four horses. Apparently they had been sacrificed and thrown in head first. In the other compartment there had been placed the cremated remains of a man and the skeleton of a woman.

The woman might have been the man's consort and could have been sacrificed at the time of his burial, for beside her head lay an iron knife with an ivory handle. The man had evidently been cremated on a huge funeral pyre, and his ashes had been placed in a bronze urn, set down near his iron sword and spear and his whetstone. The ashes had been wrapped in a cloth, and the archaeologists were astonished to find that parts of the cloth—an ankle-length robe made of linen, the upper part in a shaggy weave—were well preserved after nearly 3,000 years.

It was now clear, the archaeologists reported after the excavation, "that the structure was not a temple erected for the worship of the Olympian gods but a heroön in honor of the warrior." A *heroön* was a shrine used by a hero cult. In this case, the hero, the cremated

man, most likely of the royal family, was probably a recently deceased warrior, whom archaeologists now call the Hero of Lefkandi. His tomb proved to be the earliest such structure yet found. It would put to rest some previous conceptions of ancient Greece and bolster new archaeological insights.

Testimony to the high rank of the deceased, these horses were sacrificed and left with their chariot in a tomb in Salamis dating from the eighth century BC. Although probably made by local artisans, the horses' decorative iron and bronze trappings show distinct Egyptian and Near Eastern influences.

The Euboean finds were related to the discovery of other tombs, made two decades earlier on another large island—Cyprus—and believed to have contained local royalty. Cyprus had attracted Mycenaean migrants at the end of the Bronze Age. About 1075 BC these immigrants probably founded Salamis, a city built high on a plateau, five miles north of modern Famagusta. Excavations on Cyprus from 1956 onward have uncovered a flourishing iron- and copper-smelting industry, indicating that Cypriot metalwork, begun in the Bronze Age, had made an early transition to iron.

Cyprus would seem to have enjoyed a high standard of living right through the dark age, just as had Euboea. Although the Salamis royal burials, beginning around 750 BC, occurred nearly 200 years after those on Euboea, they reflect certain Bronze Age practices and suggest a continuity of tradition. They show, for example, that the political system of Cyprus continued to be based on the rule of local hereditary kings and attendant nobles and officials. While the common people were buried in unadorned rock-cut graves, the city's upper class was laid to rest with sumptuous pomp in a part of the necropolis reserved for the royal family and aristocracy, in the manner of Mycenaean graves.

The styles of Cypriot grave objects were wide-ranging, as they had been in Mycenaean times. The items came from Egypt, Phoenicia, Syria, Asia Minor, and Greece, especially Athens, as well as Cyprus itself. Far from sinking into isolated obscurity, Cyprus, during this bleak period, evidently lay at the hub of a network of trade and influence that stretched well beyond the Aegean.

The most magnificent of the Salamis graves is Tomb 79, a rectangular structure formed by two huge blocks of stone, topped with a gabled roof and fronted by a monumental entrance. When archaeologists opened the grave, they found among the furniture three thrones and a bed that had been made of wood and elaborately decorated with ivory plaques. One throne and its stool were covered in thin sheets of silver dotted with silver nails, suggesting the "silver-studded" throne mentioned by the eighth-century BC poet Homer in the *Iliad*. Another was decorated in a style reminiscent of the throne of Penelope, queen of Ithaca, as described in the *Odyssey* and mentioned in tablets written in Linear B found in Mycenaean palaces.

All the royal burials at Salamis entailed the sacrifice of pairs of yoked horses, calling to mind the funeral of Patroclus, friend of the hero Achilles in the *Iliad*. In Tomb 79 the archaeologists found that the grave had been used twice, once at the end of the eighth century BC to inter a royal male, and again, not long afterward, to house another royal personage. On both occasions, laid to rest with the cadavers was a team of four horses and a chariot whose wheels were fixed with linchpins almost two feet long. The inclusion of horse and chariot was a mark of the exalted status of the deceased men. Not only had animal sacrifice taken place in this tomb but human sacrifice as

Its wooden frame disintegrated (above), *this ivory throne was found at the same site as were the horses and chariot on the opposite page. Restored* (right), *with its thin gold sheets and decorative Egyptian-style plaques of a sphinx and a lotus flower in place, the throne recalls the splendor of ancient Salamis.*

well, indicated by a skeleton found with hands tied in front of the body. Other graves at Salamis demonstrated that a number of the dead were cremated in the Greek mainland tradition, which was not the usual custom on Cyprus but similar to burial practices described in the funerals of the great heroes in the *Iliad*. This was further borne out by offering jars of oil found in the graves and by fragments of the shrouds that had wrapped ashes in some of the urns.

The Salamis burials, similar to the ones on Euboea but discovered some 20 years earlier, gave rise to considerable speculation. Scholars wondered whether they could have been influenced by the *Iliad* and other epic poetry written by Homer and his fellow bards at about the same time as the interments took place. Or perhaps the reverse was the case, and Homer was reflecting a prevailing burial practice, a style and ritual that sprang from an older tradition. It was not until the later find of the hero's tomb at Euboea that the evidence favored one theory over the others. The Euboea burial seemed to undercut the argument of those who believed in the influence of the *Iliad*, for it had occurred about 950 BC, considerably before Homer's epic poetry, which was created about 750 BC. Many scholars now assume that the Euboea and Cyprus burials both provide examples of an ongoing practice of giving prominent individuals a hero's burial.

If Euboea and Cyprus recovered early from the post-Mycenaean turmoil, the island of Crete, which had dominated the Aegean throughout the Bronze Age, could not have been far behind. And indeed this proved to be the case. Nearly 1,000 feet up on a high and almost inaccessible peak in the east-central region of the island, well out of the way of the troubles on the plains below, citizens of Crete's mixed Minoan-Mycenaean culture, late in the 12th century BC, found refuge. They may have been driven there by an invasion that displaced them from their homes. Here, on their remote, hidden slope they built a town known today as Karphi.

Shortly before World War II, Karphi's remains were excavated by British archaeologists. The digs revealed the layout of a sprawling settlement that might have housed some 3,500 people. One-story houses were crudely constructed of blocks of split limestone piled one on top of the other without foundations, bonding, or plaster. The roofs were flat, with broken jars for chimneys. But there were signs of lingering sophistication: Well-placed roads ran through the town, and in the most defensible area rose a building complex archaeolo-

RELICS OF AN ACTIVE CULT CENTER

While digging in a church-owned field one day in 1929, the village priest at Ajia Irini, on the northwest coast of Cyprus, uncovered some curious terra-cotta sculptures. He showed his finds to officials at the Cyprus Museum, and soon some Swedish archaeologists, who had been working on Cyprus since 1927, were called in to examine the site in detail.

The archaeologists' excavations disclosed more than 2,000 terra-cotta statues of various sizes, all of them facing a smooth, oval-shaped stone resting on an altar. At the time of discovery the figures were somewhat disarrayed *(top right)*, but it was clear that they had been arranged in semicircles according to size, the smallest in front, the largest to the rear—as half were later displayed in a Stockholm museum *(bottom right)*.

The priest had stumbled upon a center of cult worship that dated to 1200 BC, but which had flourished from about 650 to 500 BC, when the site was all but covered over by flood-borne silt. Presumably, the statues had been emplaced by citizens as proxies for themselves, to stand as perpetual worshipers of the cult's fertility-god deity—whose name remains unknown.

gists call the Great House, the residence of Karphi's ruler, complete with megaron, or throne room, a relic of Mycenaean times. At the highest spot was a sanctuary with an altar and a bench for displaying the ceramic goddesses that archaeologists unearthed there.

For more than a century and a half this isolated refugee settlement struggled on. Then around the 10th century, conditions on Crete evidently improved enough to lure the inhabitants of Karphi to the lowlands. Their mountain stronghold was abandoned, and by the end of the 10th century, grave objects show that the island was once again in contact with the outside world. The cultural and economic upturn that had brought the Cretans down from Karphi signaled great changes throughout the Greek world as people gradually drifted back to the islands and towns previously abandoned.

The scattered villages of the depressed era began a process that the Greeks call *synoikismos,* the union of individual towns under a single capital. In Sparta and Corinth, villages within a geographically defined region sharing mutual interests joined their boundaries to create a single urban unit. In Attica, according to ancient tradition, the villages agreed to become satellites of their most important center—Athens. This was the first step toward what would become the characteristic political entity of Hellenic Greece—the city-state, a complex that included a city and its environs, ruling itself without formal ties to any outside political structure.

Between 850 and 750 BC city-states proliferated. Some estimates put their number as high as 700. Ancient writers of a later period, such as Herodotus, Strabo, and Diodorus, described the way city-states were governed, probably drawing their information from oral traditions, some of which have since been corroborated by the archaeological investigation of grave sites. Several city-states were ruled by monarchs in the manner, if not on the scale, of the great kings of the Mycenaean era. With the passing of time, the autocratic power of these monarchs waned in the face of competition from their nobles and was gradually replaced by the group rule of an oligarchy, an assembly of aristocrats based on families and organized by tribes.

Shortly before 850 BC sea routes began opening up again and a few small-scale sea traders started to establish trading posts, or emporiums, overseas. At home the demand for metals, raw materials, and foodstuffs grew. These products could be acquired by the exchange of Greek manufactured objects. Soon many Greeks turned their attention abroad, where the emporiums they were founding would shortly become rich and powerful colonies. By the eighth century Greek colonists had settled on the Aegean islands and the coasts of Asia Minor, then pushed onward to northern Syria, Phoenicia, and Palestine. Digs throughout these regions have yielded evidence of Greek visits.

Trade and colonization seem generally to have been initiated privately, not by the rulers of the city-states. While the quest for trading opportunities was a prime motivation for the movement overseas, there was also a political impetus. Colonies were often established by *oikists,* meaning founders, usually ambitious tribal aristocrats who were able to provide the leadership and investment in ships and supplies necessary for a major venture abroad. By the eighth century the oikists were keenly aware that their inherited power was being eroded by the rise of *tyrants,* a Phoenician word, referring to arbitrary, but not necessarily malign, despots. For some oligarchs, sailing off to reestablish their leadership in a new land seemed a solution to a political impasse. One scholar speculates that Homer's *Odyssey* depicts the point of view of the oikists. In the epic adventures of Odysseus's wanderings in the lands of the western Mediterranean, the western regions are seen as perilous and mysterious but also temptingly fertile. It may be that the bard was stirred by the stories of those returning from the promising new area.

Not all colonists went voluntarily: Some inhabitants of the volcanic Aegean island of Thera were shipped off to Cyrenaica (eastern Libya today) because of drought at home. They were chosen by lot and stoned when they tried to return. In Africa they prospered. Some Spartans were dispatched, against their will, to found Tarentum (now lying beneath present-day Taranto on the shore of the heel

The partially excavated site of Karphi, a town founded on Crete in the late 12th century BC, is visible on this barren mountainside in the east-central region of the island. Just who lived here and why, no one can be certain; the population is estimated at 3,500. The mystery is compounded by the fact that the inhabitants occupied the desolate spot for no more than 150 years, then went away, leaving the effigies of their goddesses.

of southern Italy); they were illegitimate children who, growing up to discover they had no civic rights, had become troublemakers. The inhabitants of Chalcis, on the island of Euboea, beset by famine, sent one-tenth of their number to found Rhegium, at the toe of Italy.

As the population grew, presumably putting pressure on food supplies and other natural resources, the diaspora from Greece soon became a flood, with Greeks settling from the northern shores of the Black Sea to Africa, from the borders of Mesopotamia in the east to France and Spain in the west. From 750 BC until well into the sixth century, many of these colonies sent out their own representatives to found additional cities in turn. In the west, the emigrants' first target was Italy. One of their earliest footholds was a trading post secured by men from Euboea on the fertile little island of Pithecusae, northwest of what is now the Bay of Naples. More than 1,300 tombs have been excavated there since 1952, revealing that most of the new arrivals were relatively humble folk from the lower classes.

Toward the end of the eighth century the Euboean settlers felt emboldened to cross over to Cumae on the Italian mainland, and by 725 BC this new trading post had become an independent colony. Early in the 20th century archaeologists exploring ancient Cumae uncovered a tomb, dating from the period of Euboean occupation, that differed strikingly from the tombs found at Pithecusae. Inside the archaeologists found the ashes of men and women interred with prized silver ornaments, iron weapons, and bronze vessels. In fairly short order the humble settlers of Cumae had ap-

Hewn into rock by Greek colonists at Cumae, in southern Italy, Sibyl's Grotto is illuminated by light shafts. The 427-foot-long chamber was carved in the fifth century BC as a place for a prophetess of the god Apollo to dispense her oracles. Figures advancing from dark to light would have disappeared and reappeared, heightening the mystery of the place.

parently evolved a noble warrior class, whose members were laid to rest according to the burial rituals of the Greek homeland.

Cumae was famed for prophesy, as ancient Greek and Roman authors have made clear. Its oracular messages were delivered by an awe-inspiring sibyl, a seeress whose words were believed to be responses from the god Apollo. In the 1920s archaeologists excavated a cave known by tradition as the grotto of the sibyl. There they came upon vaulted chambers and galleries, cut through solid rock near the top of a bluff above the sea. The abode of the oracle, according to Strabo, lay in a settlement of copper miners known as Cimmerians, who lived in underground houses and visited one another through tunnels. Ultimately the Cimmerians were slaughtered by a king who was displeased with the sibyl's message. The archaeologists identified the cave as indeed the sibyl's dwelling place.

From small beginnings Greek colonies rapidly spread throughout southern Italy. Arriving by ship, the Greeks occupied a stretch of shoreline, built homes and temples, and walled the town about. They divided the land, tilled the soil, and founded trade and industries. Inevitably colonies quarreled with colonies, going to war to settle differences. Some triumphed, others were destroyed. Southern Italy came to be called Magna Graecia, or Great Greece, for the number of Greek settlements it supported. Many—Poseidonia, Croton, and Sybaris—went on to achieve distinction, as did Gela, Syracusae (Syracuse), and Acragas (Agrigento) in nearby Sicily.

Sybaris, on the Gulf of Taranto in present-day Calabria, is remembered today for its riches; indeed, its very name has become a synonym for ultraluxurious living—sybaritic. Colonists from the Peloponnese had founded this city around 720 BC on a site between two rivers—the Sybaris (now the Coscile) and the Crathis (Crati)—in a low fertile area still known as the plain of Sibari. As the new colony grew rich and powerful, it expanded its influence until it controlled four tribes and 25 cities in southern Italy and could call some 300,000 men to arms from all over its far-flung territory.

Sybaris became known for the wealth of its wheatlands and the excellence of its wine; such historians as Strabo and Diodorus, writing long after the city was destroyed, described its opulence, extravagance, and ease of living, making legends of the lifestyle of the inhabitants. To provide themselves with wine on tap, it was said, the Sybarites laid pipelines down to the seaside port where they kept their wine cellars and had the wine pumped across the plain and into their homes. To avoid getting wet when it rained, they erected covers over the streets. Averse to early rising, they had all roosters banished to the edge of town so people would not be wakened by crowing at daybreak. Workers in noisy jobs—blacksmiths, for example—were banned from residential districts for the same reason. So lavish were the public festivities in Sybaris that invitations supposedly had to be sent out 12 months in advance to give the ladies time to prepare their sumptuous couture. The Sybarites were the butt of all sorts of tales and jokes. The sight of manual labor was so unsettling to Sybarites, goes one story, that a patrician suffered a rupture the first time he set eyes on it, and a friend got a stitch in his side just from hearing about it.

The sybaritic lifestyle came to a halt in 510 BC, when Sybaris was attacked by an army from nearby Croton, in one of those endless bouts of intercity rivalry that bedeviled the Greek colonies in Italy. One traditional story suggests that it was the Sybarites' own sophistication that contributed to their city's downfall. Their cavalry had taught their horses to dance to music, and the Crotons knew this. Croton spies infiltrated the city and memorized the tunes. At a critical juncture in the Croton advance on the city, army musicians struck up the key melodies on their pipes, and the squadrons of Sybarite chargers obligingly waltzed off the field of battle, leaving the city defenseless and doomed. Strabo said the Crotons sacked the city and then drowned it by diverting a nearby river.

Italian archaeologists tried repeatedly to find the remains of Sybaris between the 1870s and the 1930s, but in vain. The immense area that had to be searched was a daunting 450 square miles. Most of the land was marsh, formed by the flood plains of its rivers, and digging here was like delving into quicksand. Ultimately the task proved beyond the know-how then available.

It was the technology of the space age that finally enabled scientists to make a breakthrough. In 1960 a team under the Italian archaeologist Carlo Lerici resumed the quest. Adopting relatively new geological techniques, the group used electronic sound sensors to probe beneath the surface. The process involves sending low frequency radar into the ground and measuring the echoes that bounce back. Variations indicate the depth of the layer the impulses have

THE STATE OF HEALTH IN METAPONTO

The bustling Greek colony of Metaponto, on Italy's southern coast, was renowned for its wealth and the skill of its doctors. So when scientists set out to conduct

detailed health studies of many of the hundreds of undisturbed skeletons discovered there in 1982, they expected to find that the ancient Metapontians had lived long, healthy lives. Instead, the investigators found widespread evidence of disease, including malaria, malnutrition, and untreated injuries.

Under the direction of archaeologist Joseph C. Carter of the University of Texas at Austin, physical anthropologists Maciej Henneberg and Renata Henneberg of South Africa's University of the Witwatersrand excavated and studied the remains of 272 people who had lived in the prosperous Metaponto area between 600 and 250 BC. The average adult life expectancy, they determined, was 39 years for females, 42 for males. Ringlike bands of thinned tooth enamel indicated that more than 75 percent of the population had suffered disease or severe malnutrition during childhood. Tooth decay and other dental ailments were rampant, leading the researchers to conclude that dental hygiene was unknown to Metapontians.

The best-preserved skeleton was that of a 40- to 45-year-old man called "the musician" for the tortoise-shell lyre found at his left knee *(left)*. He was unusually tall—about five feet, 10 inches —for his day, and enlarged bone ends led researchers to conclude his stature may have been caused by an overactive pituitary gland. His teeth showed signs of childhood illness and malnutrition.

The most graphic instance of untreated injury was the twisted thighbone *(above)* of a man in his fifties. The bone had been broken in two places and never set but healed well enough so the man could still walk—although his leg would have been shortened by about four inches.

passed through and whether it consists of rock, clay, or sand. In the first season Lerici's team discovered a masonry wall nearly a hundred yards long and promptly announced that it indicated the remains of a large city.

These ruins, however, belonged not to Sybaris but were part of an ancient wall first built by the Greeks and later improved by the Romans to hold back the slowly encroaching sea. Then in 1961 a team from the University of Pennsylvania under Froelich G. Rainey joined the Lerici Foundation in a joint search for the elusive city. The Americans brought with them a plethora of technological tools. Their main aim was, according to Rainey, "to test and develop electronic instruments for archaeological surveys." In addition, the expedition put a multidisciplinary team in the field.

From the geologist and hydrologist's joint survey it seemed that Sybaris might lie as much as 20 feet beneath the surface—beyond the range of the electronic sounding apparatus. This study showed that Sybaris's demise was brought about not by the Crotons flooding the city, as Strabo had reported but rather by an earthquake that occurred not long after the city's capture. The quake caused a lengthy stretch of the Gulf of Taranto's coast to sink while a huge tidal wave swept in, flooding the coastal ports and inland towns, among them Sybaris. The city was engulfed by a lagoon that slowly silted up with mud brought down by the two rivers, causing all traces of the settlement to vanish under the sediment.

In 1962 the Americans brought to the site a more advanced kind of electronic equipment—a proton magnetometer. The effectiveness of this portable device is based on the fact that the earth has a magnetic field. Sensitive to changes in magnetic intensity, the instrument scans the ground and registers even the slightest variations beneath the surface. Instead of digging a trench, the investigators could bore a single hole in any one area to determine the detected anomaly, which in the deep clay plain usually indicated an archaeological feature. With the help of this instrument, the teams surveyed nearly eight square miles, made over 850 bore holes, unearthed some 10,000 archaeological fragments, located tombs, sculptures, and pottery, and indeed found a buried city. But, alas, it was not Sybaris but the more shallowly buried Roman city of Copia, which in a later period had grown up close by the vanished Sybaris.

The scientists believed the proton magnetometer could not probe deeply enough to detect Sybaris. It was not until a magnetometer using cesium, an extremely reactive metal, was brought into the study in 1967 that a breakthrough occurred. The cesium magnetometer had been developed for the space industry and was used in satellites to detect magnetic fields in space. Adapted for archaeological use, it could probe the earth to a depth of 20 feet or more and penetrate subsurface water. Capable of surveying up to 10 acres of land a day, the electronic device was sensitive enough to pinpoint a vase, tile, or length of iron on a stone floor deep in the ground.

By 1968 the cesium magnetometer had located the foundations of several large buildings, one 300 feet long, buried deep in the mud. Confident Sybaris had been found at last "beyond a reasonable doubt," Rainey and his colleagues returned the following year to continue the investigation of the site with the help of infrared aerial photography. This heat-based scanning equipment was used to plot the topography of the site. After studying the electronically produced maps, the archaeologists determined on a waterlogged location. Then they used a technique known as the wellpoint system. Pumping water out of the chosen area, to a depth of 18 feet, they were afterward able to conduct a dry excavation, and they cleared part of a theater. They could then reconstruct the town plan and retrace the Greek harbor and one of the sixth-century BC residential quarters.

While colonization and trade accelerated in the seventh century BC, a growing flood of goods from the East—metalwork, carved ivory, trinkets, and textiles—poured into Greece and its colonies. The traffic was not confined to merchandise. People, too, came and went between Greece and the cities of the East, carrying with them new ideas, especially in the arts. Contact with the Egyptians, for example, would revolutionize Greek architecture and monumental sculpture.

The fifth-century BC Greek historian Herodotus tells of Greeks forced onto the Egyptian coast by storms at sea and taken into the service of the pharaoh Psammetichos I. They were rewarded with land in the Nile Valley and became the first foreigners to settle in Egypt. For years afterward the main Greek role in Egypt seems to have been a military one. In 591 BC Psammetichos II sent an expedition up the Nile to push back Nubian forces threatening Upper

Taken from a balloon tied to the boat at upper left, this aerial photo and others like it not only helped define the extent of the submerged ruins of Halieis on the southern coast of Greece but also let archaeologists work out a grid system for systematically investigating them. Seen here are the outlines of the town's Apollo sanctuary. Halieis, which flourished from the seventh to the fourth century BC, was gradually flooded until much of it lay under more than 10 feet of water.

Egypt. Greek mercenaries accompanied the expedition to Abu Simbel, Ramses II's grand monument, where they carved inscriptions on the legs of the giant statues hewn out of the sandstone cliffs—eloquent testimony to the Greek involvement in this military venture. One inscription, for example, was "written by Archon son of Amoibichos and Pelekos son of Eudamos," on behalf of soldiers who "went as far upstream as they could." Potasimto, an Egyptian general, "led the foreigners and Amasis the Egyptians."

In subsequent years Amasis became pharaoh and conceded land to his Greek troops. Herodotus, writing a century later, records that Amasis "gave them Naucratis as a commercial headquarters for any who wished to settle in the country. He also made land grants upon which Greek traders, who did not want to live permanently in Egypt, might erect altars and sanctuaries." Naucratis became the major Greek trading town on a branch of the Nile, but its location was lost to modern scholars.

In 1883 the British archaeologist Sir Flinders Petrie visited the famous pyramids of the Giza Plateau. Offered for sale there was an alabaster figure of a soldier wearing a helmet and armlets, clearly Greek. Petrie bought it, and a few months later he went to the region alleged to be its source, some 50 miles south of present-day Alexandria. "There I met a sight almost too strange to believe," he later wrote. "Before me lay a long low mound of town ruins, of which all the core had been dug out by the natives for earth, thus baring the very lowest level of the town." Wherever he walked in this crater, Petrie found himself stepping on pieces of ancient Greek pottery.

Filling his pockets with scraps of vases and statuettes, Petrie left, returning to dig the next season. The mound was some two miles from the Egyptian village of el-Niqrash, a name that suggested the Greek settlement of Naucratis, reported by Herodotus, and other clues in the ancient text fit as well. Petrie was able to form a plan of the streets and houses. "The street lines were distinguished by the rubbish thrown out, mostly remains of food, shells, and bones," he reported. Petrie's excavation laid bare temples, sanctuaries, a storehouse, a small factory for the manufacture of faience scarab seals, a few houses, and a great deal of pottery with inscriptions in early Ionic writing. His finds persuaded scholars that Naucratis had been founded before the sixth-century BC date assigned by Herodotus, for the earliest pottery found there was Corinthian, 630 to 620 BC. Recent digs in the area, however, have raised questions as to whether Petrie's city is, in fact, Naucratis.

Herodotus had visited the ancient town and provided a broad picture of life there. The main commodity the Greeks sought in Egypt was wheat. In return for grain, the Greek merchants in Naucratis traded olive oil, wine, and silver. The community was evidently large and wealthy. The town became a magnet for get-rich-quick Greek entrepreneurs and for glittering visits by writers such as Aristophanes, the comic dramatist, and politicians such as Solon the lawgiver, as well as ladies of fortune and dubious reputation, including one Rhodopis. Rhodopis was taken there by a vintner-cum-pimp called Charaxos, brother of the renowned Lesbian poetess Sappho. Thanks to her charms, Rhodopis amassed considerable wealth in Egypt and donated a tenth of it to Apollo at Delphi, where part of the inscribed base bearing her dedication has been unearthed.

"For some reason or other," commented Herodotus, "Naucratis must be a good place for beautiful prostitutes." Perhaps the reason was the Greek males' inability to attract Egyptian women. "No Egyptian man or woman will kiss a Greek," Herodotus recorded, "or use a Greek knife, spit or cauldron, or even eat the flesh of a bull known to be clean, if it has been cut with a Greek knife."

When the Greeks ventured into Egypt and saw the soaring structures of the royal cities of the Nile Valley, they grasped the concept of monumental architecture and gigantic sculpture. It was not architectural design so much as the material and scale—the imposing dimensions carried out in stone—that they eagerly emulated. Before the Greeks came into contact with Egyptian culture, the basic plan of the Greek temple had been well established—a rectangle, with columns along the front, sides, and back and usually in double rows down the interior of the main room, which housed a cult image. To the rear there could be a treasury for donations to the god, and an altar stood before the door. The walls were typically mud brick, the roof mud covered or thatched, and the columns wood.

By 600 BC, however, after Greeks had been exposed to Egyptian monumental architecture, they began to construct their temples entirely of stone. Two architectural motifs, or orders, evolved—the Ionic in eastern Greece, which today is part of Turkey, and the Doric in the area inhabited by the Dorians on the Greek mainland. Each order was characterized by stylistic differences in the treatment of columns, bases, capitals, and other architectural elements. The sturdy Doric column was much plainer than the lighter, slimmer, and more decorated Ionic. A many-columned Temple of Artemis was built at Ephesus to demonstrate the severe beauties of the Ionic. The earliest Doric examples—at Corinth and Olympia and on the island of Corfu, a Corinthian colony—show a much stronger Egyptian influence in their capitals and decorative moldings.

The new stone buildings were to be graced with stone sculptures of the gods, goddesses, and mythical heroes. These freestanding figures first appeared in Greece in the seventh century and derived from Eastern prototypes. But with Greek imagination let loose on alien content, something wonderful happened: The Greek sense of line and balance came into play. This synthesis was most dramatically expressed in the development of the kouros (kouroi in the plural), the life-size statue of the male nude, and its draped female equivalent, the kore (korai in the plural). At first glance these figures look Egyptian in their archetypal stiffness. But the treatment of the body, the increasingly fluid stance, and the enigmatic archaic "smile" are essentially Greek. The so-called smile, however, some scholars believe does not express the subject's state of mind but rather an early attempt by Greek artists to model the structure of the lower face—a conventional method of sculpting the jaw that persisted for some time.

By the end of the century the Greeks had sufficiently mastered the rendering of the body to produce kouroi that were anatomically exact, dynamically fluid, harmonious in proportion, and naturalistic in shape. In creating the korai at a time when the conven-

The Arab trader who sold this Greek figurine to British archaeologist Sir Flinders Petrie in 1883 revealed where it had been found; Petrie trekked to the site in the Nile Delta and discovered a lost Greek settlement of the seventh century BC. In this early experiment with archaeological photography, the inventive Petrie used a mirror to show the object front and back.

tions of Greek society could not accommodate the display of female nudity, the draping of garments were as much of a challenge to the sculptor as the supple body that lay beneath them.

The western colonies greatly benefited from the new artistic ferment as evidenced by the retrieval of a series of beautifully carved metopes dating from the archaic period, the term used by some art historians to designate the years preceding the classical period. After much sleuthing, the plaques were found in scattered locations near Poseidonia, an ancient Greek city in southern Italy, today known as Paestum. Poseidonia grew rich enough to erect three resplendent temples, two of them dating from the late archaic and a third from the classical period that followed. A few miles to the north of these the Greeks had built a sanctuary in about 575 BC, dedicated to the goddess Hera. Infested with malaria-carrying mosquitoes, the site was seldom visited in modern times.

In 1934 two dedicated Italian archaeologists, Paola Zancani-Montuoro and U. Zanotti-Bianco, set out to excavate the sanctuary. Privately funded, they labored against enormous obstacles. There were no roads to the overgrown, snake-infested site, and the investigators were without a derrick or any transport except oxcarts. The archaeologists developed malaria and pneumonia, but recovering, they went on to locate the Doric frieze, with its sculptured sandstone metopes, carved for the sanctuary's treasury. The challenge of tracking down the metopes took time. Almost all of the blocks had been reused in other buildings in distant localities, so the archaeologists studied clues to their whereabouts in historic texts. When Italy went to war in 1940, the best of Zancani-Montuoro and Zanotti-Bianco's work force left to join the army. These frustrations did not deter the Italians, who eventually recovered 32 huge sandstone metopes and fragments of still another. But their problems were not over. Only ruins of three of the four treasury walls remained, allowing the width of the building to be determined, but not its precise length, and complicating the process of determining the place each metope had occupied on the treasury frieze. As the war continued, the men stored their finds in a hut on the site, and fortunately, these escaped damage and looting. Ironically, 11 of the sandstone blocks were unfinished; their creation, it is believed, had also been interrupted by military conflict, as one coalition of Greek colonies fought another.

Eighteen of the metopes took the exploits of Heracles as their

ENIGMA OF A SMILING STATUE

There are two ways of looking at the so-called Getty kouros, or young man *(right)*. It is an outstanding example of ancient Greek statuary, or it is a monumental modern fraud.

The statue was authenticated and bought—for some nine million dollars—in the mid-1980s by the J. Paul Getty Museum in Malibu, California. Its origins came into question in 1986, when a document attesting that it had once belonged to a Swiss collector was exposed as a forgery.

Intensive studies followed. Unlike a known fake that the museum obtained for the purpose of comparison *(far right, top)*, the Getty kouros showed no telltale markings of modern tools or signs of artificial aging of the surface. On the other hand, art historians pointed out that the Getty sculpture features a highly unlikely combination of physical characteristics—such as hair style and the anatomical naturalness of feet and hands—that had in fact varied from region to region and evolved over time.

The final verdict is inconclusive. Scientists call the figure authentic, while most art historians dub it a fraud. And the truth remains as enigmatic as the expression on the statue's stone face.

The inadvertent hallmark of a careless modern forger, this hand print was left on the fake kouros when the figure's maker applied an iron-rich compound to simulate aging.

An ultraviolet photograph of the bogus kouros (far left) reveals a uniform surface inconsistent with long contact with the earth (the statue's head, a plaster replica, shows up more brightly under ultraviolet light). The Getty kouros (left) displays a complex pattern of mineral and organic deposits.

Shown magnified 830 times, the irregular surface crust of the Getty kouros (right) is consistent with that of a naturally weathered statue. The mineral-rich, brownish deposit—which could have been left on the work by clay—suggests long burial.

Six feet, eight inches tall, the Getty kouros is typical of a type of statue sculpted in the sixth century BC. But, curiously, its hair and feet display stylistic touches peculiar to widely different times within that century.

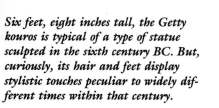

theme, and others dealt with the Trojan War and various other motifs. Fresh and bold, they revealed the refinement of the stonemasons' art and their wit as well, shown in the depiction, for example, of Odysseus riding a tortoise or centaurs, some with feet, others with hooves. Each block was sponged with sodium silicate to toughen the friable sandstone. Finally in 1952 all 32 metopes were put on display in a museum built for them at Paestum.

Although Eastern influence inspired developments in Greek architecture, it was the Phoenicians who spurred Greek literature when the Greeks adapted the Phoenician alphabet for their own use. The earliest examples of the new Greek writing are late eighth-century BC inscriptions scratched on fragments of so-called geometric pottery discovered near Athens. One such inscription, written on a jug given as a prize in a dancing competition, reads: "He whose performance is best among all the dancers shall have me."

The beginning of literacy enabled the spellbinding epic poems of the age—long passed orally from generation to generation—to be written down for the first time and preserved for future generations. And the greatest of these, of course, were Homer's.

Half a century after Homer, Hesiod produced two epics, the *Theogony,* speculating about the creation of the universe, and *Works and Days,* a verse letter to his brother, which provides a picture of the daily life on a farm around 700 BC. Hesiod emerges as a relatively prosperous farmer, who owned a draft ox, a cart, and an iron-shod plow. He lived in the village of Askra in the Boeotian highlands of central Greece. In August 1981 two British archaeologists, Anthony M. Snodgrass of Cambridge University and John L. Bintliff of Durham University, set out to make a surface survey of the Askra area. Unlike an excavation, which gives an exhaustive picture of a small place, this type of study can provide useful, if limited, information about life over a long period of time throughout a large area. It is accomplished by workers picking up from the ground all distinctive material that, from repeated plowing and the natural shifting of the earth over the centuries, has risen to the surface from the buried layers beneath. The workers identify, date, and record each scrap. From such clues archaeologists can extrapolate periods of occupation, population size, and any shifts in a settlement's development.

Snodgrass and Bintliff divided Hesiod's village into segments

The Temple of Athena at Paestum (below) was built about 570 BC and is one of the first-known structures to combine Doric and Ionic columns—a feature that was later incorporated in the Parthenon in Athens. A few miles from the temple, Italian archaeologists in 1934 discovered a trove of metopes, large decorative carvings of various mythological events. In the metope at right, the hero Heracles carries a pair of trussed-up, thieving Kerkopes, or gnomes, on the ends of a pole; amused by their coarse comments about his hairy backside, Heracles later set his captives free.

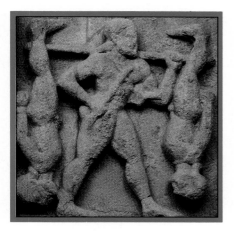

of about an acre each. Team members walked some 16 yards apart along a strip approximately five yards wide, retrieving sherds and other fragments. Then they examined intensively a smaller section of each subdivision, an area some 359 square yards, with every square yard pored over. The surveyors retrieved some 35 distinctive artifacts per acre. About half of the 2,000 artifacts gathered offered useful information, revealing that Askra had been occupied for long periods at a time, since 2500 BC. About 900 BC the town grew large enough to accommodate 1,000 or more men, women, and children, and it remained a substantial village until about AD 100.

The new literacy engendered a public demand for written laws, and committing them to stone offered a corrective to the arbitrary dictates of tyrants. The earliest of these codified laws yet found turned up in Gortyn in south central Crete, not far from one of the great Minoan palaces. In the late 19th century Italian archaeologists found a series of stone slabs along the embankment of a stream close by a mill. Excavation showed these to have been incorporated into the side of an ancient Greek theater. The blocks were inscribed with carefully hewn, well-preserved Greek letters, quite modern in appearance—square, elegant, and perfectly matched. While the tablets date from the fifth century BC, the almost biblical phrasing of the laws themselves date them back to the seventh century BC. Important legal distinctions are made, such as the cases where a judge must decide according to statutes and based on witness testimony or those where the judge can give free reign to his own perceptions and assessments.

With literacy, the Greek

prehistoric period ended. The formal marker for the beginning of the historic era is considered to be the first Olympic Games in 776 BC, in which runners, long jumpers, wrestlers, discus and javelin throwers, and racers competing from all parts of the Greek world honored Zeus. Thereafter the games took place every four years. They were not the only athletic events celebrated by the Greeks. Festivals accompanied by competitions took place regularly at Delphi, to honor Apollo, at Nemea, in honor of Zeus, and at Isthmia, on behalf of Poseidon. These were known as the crown games because winners were awarded the simple but coveted crown of leaves—an olive wreath at Olympia, laurel at Delphi, wild celery at Nemea, and pine at Isthmia. In addition there were annual games in Athens dedicated to Athena, known as the Panathenaea, where the prize was an amphora of oil from the sacred groves of the deity. The games were a major element in the growing self-awareness of Greeks as Greeks.

The festivals provided another opportunity for Greek business instincts to develop, for they were not only religious and sports events but also commercial fairs. They developed in an era of great economic innovation. By about 600 BC a new standard of wealth revolutionized trade: Coinage, which had probably originated in Sardis, capital of the wealthy kingdom of Lydia (in today's central Turkey), was introduced. However rudimentary it may have been at the time, the minting of money proved but a logical extension of the concept of "movable wealth," provided by precious metals. The oldest coins found on the Greek mainland were produced in the middle of the sixth century on the island of Aegina, in the Saronic Gulf south of Athens, and bear a sea turtle as a symbol.

During the sixth century the Greeks made ever greater strides. The city-states, though still in the main ruled by tyrants, continued to develop constitutional rights, define the obligations of citizenship, and codify laws. These crucial elements, together with the rise of a middle class, would lead to the first democracies. Colonization con-

Probably produced by a Greek artisan for a Scythian chieftain, this 16-inch hammered-gold fish turned up with a set of Scythian battle gear in a farm field near Brandenburg, Germany, in 1882. The creature's body is embellished on the top with a cryptic scene of a panther and a lion attacking a boar and a deer; at the bottom, a school of fish follows a leader with a Scythian-like human head.

tinued as the Greeks sought materials in the West, even perhaps tin for bronze production from as far away as Britain, a major source. Apparently with the metal in mind, they founded around 600 BC a settlement that they called Massilia—today the great French port of Marseilles—at the mouth of the Rhone River, down which the tin could be shipped for transport across the Mediterranean. The sea routes to western Europe were controlled by the competing Phoenicians.

The cultural impact of the Greeks on the native Gauls—a subgroup of the Celts—was considerable, not just in Massilia but across much of the south of France. As the Roman historian Justinus wrote of the Gauls: "Their progress, in manners and wealth, was so brilliant that it seemed that Gaul had become part of Greece, rather than that Greece had colonized Gaul." The archaic Ionian Greek adventurers who had founded Massilia brought to the wineless Gallic barbarians of the Rhone Valley Greek country wine imported mainly from Athens and eastern Greece. Archaeologists have unearthed evidence of Greek wine consumption in the form of wine jars in Languedoc, Provence, and along the Côte d'Azur.

In pursuit of tin, the Greeks thrust ever northward, establishing colonies and emporiums along the way. Their goods spread throughout Europe and have been excavated as far afield as Angers in France's Loire Valley, near Stockholm in Sweden, in Switzerland, and in Germany. At the same time, the peripatetic Greeks were progressing along the Adriatic and through northern Italy, Macedon, and Thrace, and penetrating along the shores of the Black Sea. Russian archaeologists have unearthed Greek pottery indicating that the Greeks congregated in two locations—on the west coast of the Black Sea, in Thracian territory, and on the north coast, in Scythian lands, where they founded, at the mouth of the Dnieper, the most northerly Greek settlement, Olbiopolis (Wealthy City), known as Olbia. Its design was copied from the Greek mother city, Miletus.

Archaeologists have carried out an extensive investigation at Olbia. Though the Black Sea has flooded much of the town's lower level, aerial photography enabled them to map the area, then excavate it. The lower town seems to have housed the greater concentration of the populace, numbering up to 10,000 in the course of time. The upper town held the principal civic sites—the marketplace, courthouse, and sacred shrines—and the homes of prosperous merchants.

A beacon of Mediterranean culture in the north, Olbia stood at the center of a complex of some 70 interlinked satellite settlements in a territory nearly 40 miles wide and 30 deep. Archaeological excavations at a settlement known as Berezan—on an island located in an estuary of the Dnieper—have thrown fascinating light on small-town life far from home. The Mediterranean immigrants of Berezan evidently found the winters so cold that they sank their single-room, thatch-roof dwellings low into the ground to survive the icy blasts.

Poking into a crack in the wall of one of the houses, archaeologists found a rolled-up sheet of lead that turned out to be a letter unread for 2,500 years. The writer complained about a claim for one of his slaves and an alleged swindle by a commercial outfit in the locality. Written in the Ionian dialect, it is the earliest Greek business letter that has come down to the modern era in its original form.

Herodotus visited Olbia in the middle of the fifth century and recorded how Olbia's goldsmiths prospered by selling gold objects with animal motifs to the indigenous Scythian tribesmen of the region (*pages 66-67*). Many of these have been found in the tombs of southern Russia. In return for grain, wheat-rich Scythia's main commodity, Greek ships brought olive oil and wine. Excavations near Olbia have revealed a dozen storage pits and a grain-drying oven.

The Greeks seemed to have got on well with their Scythian neighbors. Intermarriage was common and cultural integration relatively advanced, according to Herodotus. This probably came of expediency: The Greek settlers had to adopt a flexible and tolerant attitude toward the native populace, for Olbia was an indefensible city and the Scythians were not to be trifled with—for one thing, they scalped their enemies. And not all the indigenous population could be cajoled. The Tauri of the Crimea, said Herodotus, were prone to human sacrifice, and this included "all shipwrecked sailors and such Greeks as they happen to capture."

In this, their northern outpost, as in Asia Minor, Egypt, and Europe, the Greeks had proven themselves indomitable, talented, and dynamic. Now, entering the fifth century, they were about to launch the great classical age, the inspiration of the Western world and one of the finest periods in human history.⊠

PUBLIC AND PRIVATE LIVES

O urs is no workaday city," said the famed states-man Pericles of fifth-century BC Athens. "No other provides so many recreations of the spirit. We are lovers of beauty without extravagance, lovers of wisdom without loss of manliness. Our citizens attend both to public and private duties, allowing no absorption in their own affairs to interfere with their knowledge of the city. We yield to none, man by man, for independence of spirit, manysidedness of attainment, and complete self-reliance in limbs and brain." Allowing for rhetorical exaggeration, Pericles' oration nevertheless reflects reality, for Athenian citizens were expected to engage in politics and public speaking, serve in the army or navy, perform athletically, sing, dance, and play an instrument, marry and produce children, ply a trade, appreciate artistic beauty, and participate in religious ceremony.

Yet, in other ways, the rosy picture painted by Pericles and sustained by generations of Western historians is a romantic illusion. The total population of Athens numbered about 300,000, but only 30,000 belonged to the privileged adult-male citizen group partaking in the fledgling democratic system. The remainder were women, children, resident aliens, and slaves, all disenfranchised. And it seems that during the so-called golden age, for the average Greek the housing conditions were mean, the diet meager, and the work long and hard. Not many Athenians enjoyed the genteel luxury of the woman above, bathing in her boudoir.

Few professions were more demanding than that of potter, and indeed an ancient Greek idiomatic expression for working hard was "to make pottery." Ironically, these artisans, some of them slaves and most not eligible for citizenship, provided for posterity the greatest wealth of information about Athenian dress, home furnishings, social customs, religious practices, and athletic events. On the following pages, their painted work illustrates aspects of daily life in Athens.

THE FINISHING TOUCH: A GREEK EDUCATION

For the citizens of ancient Athens, a betrothal between a young man and a young woman began with the prospective groom saying, "I am getting married in order to have children." Children, especially boys, fulfilled the mandate of carrying on the family's line and performing civic duties. Both boys and girls spent their early childhoods at home, in the care of their mothers and household servants. Ever helpful, Greek philosophers lent their authority to theories of proper child rearing. Plato, for example, suggested that a boy would be better prepared for his eventual profession if he played with miniature tools.

Around the age of six or seven, boys began their formal schooling. Regardless of economic status, all young males gained some knowledge of the three main disciplines, music, letters, and gymnastics. The first two subjects were often combined since classical poetry was conceived originally as song. The music class below therefore combines learning to play the lyre with the recitation of a poem that starts, "O Muse, I begin to sing of broad Scamander." Other instruments and a basket for scrolls hang above the class, while a student's *paedogogos*, or slave engaged to look after a boy outside of his home, sits nearby. Girls were deemed not worthy of a formal education and (with the exception of the young women attending the school run by the iconoclastic poet Sappho, on Lesbos) were kept at home to learn domestic skills.

A typical portrayal of an Athenian child's early life, on a vase of a type given to children at an annual spring festival, renders it fairly idyllic, filled with games and toys and doting adults. Athens's infant mortality rate was high; it is estimated that one in every three babies died before the age of one.

71

A CIRCUMSCRIBED ROLE FOR WOMEN

History traditionally described respectable Athenian women as cloistered, uneducated housewives who spent their lives tending to their families' needs, spinning and weaving, and venturing into society only on prescribed religious occasions. Careful examination by scholars of fifth-century vase paintings, however, presents a slightly different picture of the everyday life of Athenian wives during the classical period.

Painters depicted women carrying out many activities and duties, including childcare and weaving. But they were shown also as gymnasts, musicians, and poets, or enjoying the outdoors, diving, swimming, and picking fruit *(below)*. Seen as occurring in the company of other women, these activities suggest a kind of parallel world of intellectual and social interaction. Such freedoms may have been available only in middle age, for the orator Hyperides said, "A woman who leaves the home ought to be at a stage of life when those who come across her don't ask whose wife she is but whose mother she is."

A woman carries a loutrophoros in a painting of a wedding scene that adorns one of the distinctively shaped vases used to hold sacred water for both Athenian nuptial and maiden death rites. Marriages, religious ceremonies, and funerals were among the few public events in which women played a major role.

73

THE HIGHLIGHT OF ATHENIAN NIGHTLIFE

The men's social gathering called a *symposion*, though often thought of as a dinner, literally meant a time of drinking together. A meal, offered early on and hurried through, simply prefaced the main event, a night of wine, music, entertainment, and conversation, serious and amusing.

Reclining on couches around the perimeter of the andron, a room reserved for men, guests were served carefully diluted libations while treated to performances by female musicians or dancers. The symposiasts often performed as well, singing, reciting poetry, and playing the lyre. At more unrestrained revels *(below)*, the men engaged in drinking games such as *kottabos*, flinging the dregs of wine from their cups at a target. And, as the painted scenes reveal, some evenings degenerated into drunken orgies.

For many participants, though, the symposion served the graver purpose of revealing a man's character through his ability to display moderation. The historian Herodotus wrote of a man who tested the suitors for his daughter's hand by gauging their behavior while drinking, one of many similar tales. Even Dionysus, the god of wine, was made to say in a play by Eubulus that after three bowls of wine, "wise guests go home."

Bawdy and ribald scenes such as this one of drunken revelers often decorated both the interior and exterior of a kylix, or drinking cup. The painted vessels were made specifically for use at symposia, each guest bringing his own.

HONING THE MIND AND BODY FOR COMPETITION

Although the Greeks were not the first to play games or sports, they were the first to elevate athletics to the status of serious competition, pitting representatives from various city-states against one another. Indeed, the word *athlete* itself comes from the Greek *athlos,* or contest. Athletic prowess, for the Greeks, was tied to military readiness and to a competitive spirit so strong that no prizes were necessary to guarantee that the fiercest effort would be put forth to win. The premiere event, the Olympic Games, offered its winners no reward beyond an olive wreath and the honor of victory.

Having started out as a simple footrace, Olympic contests eventually included discus and javelin throwing, horse and chariot racing, wrestling and boxing, and long-jumping *(below),* most done in the nude. By the fifth century BC, athletes began to specialize in certain events and hire professional trainers to oversee their preparations, to the dismay of the playwright Euripides, who stated that "the olive wreaths ought to go to the real men, who frame peace-treaties and put an end to battles and revolutions."

But the social status afforded champions and their hometowns spawned even more contests, including Athens's Panathenaea. Part religious festival and part athletic competition, the Panathenaea became a spectacular event designed to enhance and promote the city's image as foremost in power, wealth, and beauty.

Decorated with a scene of the footrace for which it was awarded, an earthenware amphora filled with sacred oil served as a trophy in the Panathenaic Games. Taken home after the games by the winners, such amphorae have turned up as far away as Marseilles and the Black Sea.

THE VALUE OF HAVING A TRADE

One of the most important responsibilities of a Greek citizen was landownership, and agriculture remained the base of the economy throughout the classical era. As the number of city dwellers steadily increased, however, tradespeople and merchants proliferated. Archaeologists excavating Athens's Agora have uncovered evidence of perfumers, potters, marble cutters, tanners, and foundry workers *(below)*, all plying their trades in and around the busy commercial center. Workshops became important gathering places, and Socrates frequented one that was owned by a cobbler named Simon.

Though slaves performed most of the manual labor, Greeks did not scorn hard work and often toiled beside their servants for the same wages. A man's wealth was measured by his self-sufficiency. As a character in one of Menander's plays remarked, "A stroke of bad luck strips you of your money. What are you left with? Just a naked body! There's only one security in life, and that's to have a trade."

Vase painters and potters work at their craft in the workshop scene that adorns this fifth-century krater, or mixing bowl. The exceptional workmanship and elegant design of its painted pottery made Athens the leading producer and exporter of ceramic wares in the Mediterranean.

THE MEANING OF IT ALL

Classical Greece enjoys a glorious reputation for the wisdom of many of its illustrious citizens, original thinkers who pursued a course of rational inquiry into the sublime philosophical questions of life. A majority of Greeks, however, seemed more inclined to accept the advice of oracles who interpreted the rustling of leaves or the entrails of sacrificed animals. Tablets found at sacred shrines revealed that pilgrims' inquiries were often personal, about work and spouses, and as Plato pointed out, people "were quite happy to believe oak trees and rocks, so long as the answers were right."

Among the omen readers, some of whom observed and construed thunder and lightning or the trills and warbles of birds, the oracle of Apollo at Delphi seemed the most trusted. Within the sanctuary of Apollo in the mountainous area northwest of Athens, the Pythia, a woman who spoke for the god, drank from the sacred spring and ate bay leaves from Apollo's tree while seated on a three-legged stool *(below)*. Thus fortified, the Pythia answered her petitioners. The presumed reliability of the Delphic oracle may be explained by the clever ambiguity of her replies. Herodotus related the story of the Lydian king Croesus, who asked the oracle if he should invade Persia. She responded that if he did, "he would destroy a great empire." The heartened Croesus attacked, but the empire he destroyed was his own.

Standing before a cult statue at a shrine, a bearded priest attended by a winged deity awaits the arrival of a bull for sacrifice. Typically, such animals were offered grain so they would bend their necks to eat and in doing so appear to be nodding in consent to their slaughter.

ATHENS: EIGHTH WONDER OF THE ANCIENT WORLD

"N ever in the history of the world," it has been written of classical Athens, "has there been such a multiplication of varied talents and achievements within so limited a period." Between 480 and 400 BC, Athenian statesmen transformed the art of political organization. Greek generals won extraordinary victories. Poets, architects, and sculptors opened avenues into the soul. And scientists and philosophers changed the very structure of human thought. Athens's power became so great, and its influence reached so far, that the period is commonly characterized as a golden age. Actually, it might more accurately be called a silver age, for as Herodotus, Xenophon, Demosthenes, and other ancient writers indicate, it was silver that made these achievements possible.

In this resource Athens was blessed. Most of the silver that filled its treasury was mined in Laurium, the rugged, hilly region located about 25 miles to the southeast of the city. Farmers have long managed to scratch a living from the plains that line Laurium's jagged coast, but archaeologists know the area inland to be one of the driest in all of Attica. No more than a few inches of rain dampen its dusty, rocky soil all year, and no rivers or streams freshen the deep valleys that part the highlands. Even stands of pines planted decades ago in a reforestation effort cannot hide the barrenness of the terrain. Slag heaps left by miners 24 centuries ago, and not trees, still number

Arms poised to bear a long-lost spear and shield, this 12-inch bronze figure of the helmeted goddess Athena—patron of the city of Athens— was found on that once-mighty Greek city's Acropolis.

among the region's chief features. Exploring these piles in 1860, Greek engineers showed that the area, long presumed to be exhausted of its metallic riches, might still be a profitable source of silver, lead, manganese, and zinc, and in 1864 the mines were reopened. The resumption of work gave scholars a unique chance to learn firsthand about the ways and means of ancient Greece, and Édouard Ardaillon, a classicist and geographer affiliated with the French School in Athens, was among those who seized the opportunity.

Not content with the reports of earlier amateur explorers, Ardaillon personally conducted an exhaustive study of the region's geology and examined, often in a crawling position, the mines from which so much wealth once issued. In addition to locating massive cisterns in which the ancient Greeks painstakingly gathered what little rain fell in the area and ingenious washeries where the precious ore was separated out from worthless sediment, Ardaillon also mapped mile after mile of mine tunnels. These reached deep into the hillside, riddling it, as one historian put it, "like wormholes in wood."

Having realized early that the ore lay in narrow bands between strata of limestone and schist, the miners followed the layers with precision, the snaking course of their tunnels traced by parallel shafts for ventilation. Few of the channels, Ardaillon learned, were more than three feet tall. Those who labored in them must have done so on their hands and knees or flat on their backs. The explorer discovered the rusted remains of their simple iron hand tools—hammers, chisels, picks, and adzes—as well as the small oil lamps with which they attempted to chase away the gloom of the interior and illuminate their arduous work.

The lamps, Ardaillon estimated, would have provided 10 hours of eerie, flickering light at a time, yet shifts longer than a couple of hours could never have been endured, for conditions surely were infernal, as two additional finds suggest. Sunk fast into the tunnel walls were iron rings for anchoring chains—a grim reminder that those who had toiled here were slaves and criminals whose condition did not have to be considered too carefully. Outside, not far from the horizontal passageways, cisterns, and washeries, stood the remains of stone structures thought to be watchtowers—suggesting mine owners may have considered the laborers a danger to security.

Ardaillon's investigations, and those of subsequent archaeologists who continue to dig at Laurium, reveal an unpleasant side of the golden age. Scholars and archaeologists alike have had to face the fact that the stunning beauty and high achievements of the world's first democracy were financed largely by the toil of people who evidently were treated little better than animals. This is only one of the paradoxes in Athens's history, for the area long languished as a backwater, a place fortune seemed to have ignored while blessing the other city-states of Greece as they emerged from the dark age. Silver may have been the means by which Athens rose to eminence, but what set it on its course? What drove Athens to the fore and to such heights?

There was little in the ninth century BC to indicate that the group of mud-brick huts that clustered around a low hill above the Aegean Sea was destined to be a great city and center of an extensive empire. Nor was there anything to suggest that the people coaxing the barest of livings from the stony fields and sparse hillsides of Attica would ever come to anything. Elsewhere, some of the hundreds of independent city-states were already benefiting from the switch from pastoral to arable farming and the development of iron metallurgy. After the middle of the eighth century BC, they began founding overseas colonies to absorb surplus population, provide raw materials, and gain partners in trade.

It is not that Athens was without advantages of its own. In a land whose mountainous terrain dictated that even internal commerce had to be conducted largely by sea, its location—halfway down the Greek landmass, where the Attic peninsula jutted into the Aegean—conferred opportunity. And commanding an area of comparatively level terrain at the heart of Attica, protected to the north by Mount Aegaleos and to the south by the hills of the Imittos Range, the township seemed an obvious focal point should the region's many scattered villages combine to form a confederation. Moreover, the land offered ready stores of fine marble and clay, resources that in the years ahead would enable its builders and potters to produce monuments and wares that still stun the world with their beauty. Yet Athens slumbered on unchanged while the city-states that would become its rivals flourished.

Explaining why Athens so long lagged behind has been a matter of debate among historians for generations. In recent decades, archaeologists from the American School of Classical Studies at Athens have uncovered evidence at the Agora, the marketplace and civic center at the heart of the city, that suggests the answer. John Camp,

the director of the school's excavations since 1987, notes that while most traces of the dark age in Athens have almost entirely disappeared, a number of clearly identifiable well shafts dating to that period have been found sunk deep into the bedrock.

From pottery fragments recovered at the bottom of these shafts, archaeologists know the wells were in use up to about 700 BC, then abruptly abandoned. Since analyses of graves of the period indicate a sharp increase in mortality, with a corresponding drop in population, Camp suggests that drought and epidemic disease dealt Attica a severe twofold blow. Such a disaster would have posed a major obstacle to development, while the resulting reduction in the number of Athenians would have obviated the need for colonization.

Those who survived lived in a society riven by class and clan rivalries. Only a few noble families who claimed descent from the region's original tribes held power, and commoners, considered second-class citizens, were denied participation in government. At the same time, an increasingly large number of inhabitants—including tenant farmers, whose huge debts to their landlords robbed them of their personal freedom as well as the fruits of their labor—lived in desperate poverty. By the beginning of the sixth century BC, the situation had become intolerable.

Looking for someone daring and resourceful to reconcile the conflicting forces, the Athenians made the general, politician, and poet Solon their chief magistrate. Pronouncing all debts canceled and debtor slaves freed, he passed laws allowing all but the poorest Athenian males to hold public office and giving all freeborn men the right to vote at the Assembly, the state's main legislative body. The reforms did not survive for long after Solon went into voluntary exile, as persistent tensions between the haves and have-nots and between those in and out of power again turned to open quarreling. So recently enfranchised, voters now cast ballots only for candidates put

Obscured by the dust of centuries and surrounded by pottery whose geometric designs date the burial to the late eighth century BC, this woman's skeleton was uncovered in the Athenian Agora. The burial had occurred some 200 years before the area became a hub of civic activity. In the archaeological drawing at right, the grave and its contents are shown in precise detail.

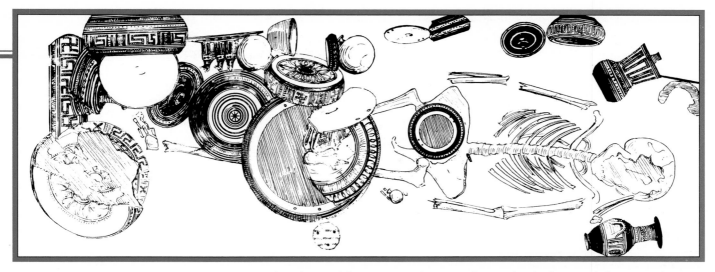

up by the nobles. But Solon's reforms had changed forever the political temper of the Athenians: Having once tasted power, they would not easily forget it.

A series of ambitious blue bloods attempted to install themselves as sole rulers, or tyrants, in the years ahead. Among them was Pisistratus, who twice seized power in Athens after 570 BC but failed to bring order to the city's chaotic economic situation and was expelled. He would not establish himself firmly in control until 545 BC, after earning enough money from silver mining in Macedon to hire an army of mercenaries to do his bidding. Once in office, Pisistratus took steps to protect trade routes connecting Athens with the wheat fields of southern Russia and timber forests of Macedon, and he embarked on a construction program aimed at solidifying his standing in the eyes of his subjects. Traces of his projects, which included an aqueduct that brought water to the capital, a temple to Dionysus, the god of wine, and a gigantic temple for Zeus, greatest of the gods, have been found in excavations.

"For the first time since the days of the Mycenean palaces," says Camp, "Athenians had the two elements necessary for monumental art: a strong centralized authority and accumulated wealth." Clearly intended to promote the tyrant's image at home and abroad, the buildings must also have bolstered the pride of ordinary Athenians and strengthened their identification with their state. Until his death in 528 BC Pisistratus was a force, if not for freedom, at least for modernization. The years of his rule were crucial to the development of the Athenian economy and the city's civic consciousness.

That the tyrant was aware of this growing sense of "Athenianism" there can be little doubt. Historians believe Pisistratus fostered it as a means of breaking the hold of aristocratic families and binding the city's different classes and factions together under his own rule. Indeed, the discovery by archaeologists of numerous inscriptions and artifacts dedicated to Athena in shrines of this date suggests her promotion as patron for Athens resulted from a carefully managed campaign designed to establish the goddess in the religious consciousness of the people. That way, Pisistratus could demote local deities with traditional ties to the city's great families.

In order to help weave reverence for Athena and love for her city into the very fabric of Athenian life, Pisistratus reorganized a spectacular festival, the Panathenaea, to be held yearly. Featuring contests of strength, speed, and skill at arms, the celebration also came to include musical competitions, recitations of Homer's epic poetry, torch racing, and even a regatta in the harbor. Every four years, a grand procession led from the Agora—which now took form as a focus for civic life—to the Acropolis. By also establishing the Dionysia, an annual contest for dramatists that was associated with a spring festival honoring the god Dionysus, Pisistratus helped to make his city a center for culture and the arts, driving home still more firmly the message of Athens's unique identity.

Despite these accomplishments, Pisistratus's regime was to crumble under his sons Hipparchus and Hippias. Hipparchus was assassinated while marshaling the Panathenaic procession in 514 BC, prompting Hippias to turn Athens into a virtual police state. His harsh rule poisoned the public goodwill that had sustained his father, and in 510 BC Hippias was deposed. Far from saddened by these events, the Athenians marked the tyrants' overthrow by erecting statues of Hipparchus's assassins in the Agora and conferring upon their descendants the great honor of being fed at public expense for life.

The Athenian nobles tried

Huge paving stones still mark this section of the Panathenaic Way, which linked the Agora to the Acropolis. In addition to carrying everyday traffic between these two important points in Athens, the 1,093-yard thoroughfare served as a ceremonial boulevard for great civic and religious festivals.

In a section of the Parthenon frieze—now displayed in the British Museum—horsemen troop along the Panathenaic Way during the Great Panathenaea, a festival of thanksgiving held every four years in honor of Athena.

to resume their old fractious ways, but thanks to the efforts of Cleisthenes, the head of a noble house that had supported Solon, their attempts failed. Between 506 and 500 BC, Cleisthenes returned to every freeborn adult male the right to participate in the Assembly and created a steering committee called the boule to shape the legislative body's agenda. In a radical break with tradition, the boule's 500 members were chosen according to place of residence rather than genealogy, putting aristocrats and commoners on equal footing for the first time. To guard against corruption, the representatives were limited to only two one-year terms, and the citizen members of the Assembly were granted the authority to ostracize, or exile, officials thought to be too powerful.

What is known today as democracy—that is, rule by the demos, or people—was born. Defined by the fourth-century BC philosopher Aristotle as requiring "the election of officers by all out of all; and that all should rule over each, and each in his turn over all," the system would serve Attica well for the next 200 years, but as the sixth century gave way to the fifth, forces were already gathering to test it.

At that time, nearly half the Greek-speaking world—including all of Asia Minor and the north coast of the Aegean as far west as Macedon—lay under Persian domination. Resentful of the taxes flowing into Persian coffers, the Greek upper class incited rebellion in the east, and Athens and Eretria, a city on the island of Euboea, went so far as to lend soldiers to an assault on Sardis, the former capital of Lydia. Angered by such meddling, the Persian king Darius ordered Miletus, the Ionian city that sparked the revolt, laid to waste and sent a mighty army to punish the homeland Greeks.

After savaging Eretria in the summer of 490 BC, the Persians landed at Marathon, on the east coast of Attica, and made ready for what they assumed would be an easy and decisive march on Athens, only 26 miles away. But before the invaders could attack, they were met in battle by a woefully outnumbered but highly motivated Athenian army and defeated.

The victory catapulted democratic Athens into a position of leadership in the Greek world and cast other city-states—including Sparta, since the middle of the sixth century the greatest city in southern Greece—into its shadow. A conservative warrior state, Sparta had always viewed Athens's political experiments with suspicion. That the Athenians' triumph now gave them first place in Greece's military order caused such resentment that it would simmer for decades before boiling over into the Peloponnesian War, which pitted the two city-states against each other and raged from 432 BC until Athens's submission in 404 BC.

For the moment, however, Athens was riding high, its economy booming as demand surged throughout the eastern Mediterranean for its olive oil and other exports. A flood of silver from Laurium, where in 483 BC a rich vein of ore had been struck, added to the windfall. The Assembly debated whether the surplus should be struck into 10-drachma coins and distributed among the citizens. But persuaded by Themistocles, one of the city's chief administrators and one of its most colorful and compelling figures, the Athenians instead put the money to a more practical end. They built a fleet of triremes— small, sturdy warships equipped with sails for traveling long distances and three tiers of oars to be used in battle *(pages 94-95)*.

"He was," the Greek historian Plutarch observed of Themistocles some six centuries later, "the only man who had the courage to come before the people and propose that the revenue from the silver mines at Laurium, which the Athenians had been in the habit of dividing among themselves, should be set aside and the money used to build triremes."

Themistocles' shipbuilding program would prove foresightful, for storm clouds were again gathering on the far shores of the Aegean. Having assembled the greatest armed force the world had ever seen, the new Persian king Xerxes, Darius's son, set out to avenge his father's defeat at Marathon. In

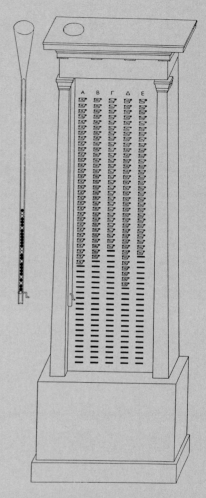

CHOOSING A JURY AT RANDOM

Of all the civic functions that citizens of Athens were called upon to perform, few were more vital to the maintenance of democracy than jury duty. And the Athenians devised an ingenious apparatus to ensure that jurors were chosen at random and from among all of the 10 geography-based administrative units—known as *phylai,* or tribes—that the populist leader Cleisthenes had established toward

the end of the sixth century BC when he abolished the old system of hereditary rule.

Athenian juries consisted of at least 201 and as many as 2,500 men. (Athenian women had neither the same rights nor the same responsibilities as the men in civic matters.) Every year, each potential juror received a bronze ticket, or *pinakion (below),* inscribed with his name, his father's name, and his *deme,* or village of origin. On trial days, he appeared at court, approached 10 baskets corresponding to Athens's tribes, and dropped the ticket into the one representing his. A magistrate would then take tickets from the first basket and insert them in the first column of slots in a wooden device like the one shown at left. (In actual use, a pair of such five-column devices would be placed side by side to accommodate the 10 tribes.) Tickets from the second basket would be put in the second column, and so on until each column was filled.

Inserted at the side of the machine was a bronze tube topped by a funnel. The magistrate would place in the funnel a mix of black and white marbles, which would fall randomly into the tube. At the turn of a crank at the bottom of the tube, marbles would drop one at a time: If a white marble appeared, the 10 citizens whose tickets were in the first row would be seated on the jury; a black marble would dismiss for the day the citizens in that row. The magistrate would continue cranking out black and white marbles until the jury was filled and ready to deliberate a case. Using this system, Athenians sought to ensure fairness in their judicial proceedings.

480 BC his army—comprising hundreds of thousands of Medes, Bactrians, Indians, Ethiopians, and Ionian Greeks as well as Persians—poured across Thrace and Macedon in the north and, escorted by a massive fleet of Phoenician, Cypriot, Egyptian, and other warships, made its way south along the coast of Thessaly.

Despite heroic resistance from the Spartans, who agreed to set aside their differences with the Athenians in order to meet the common threat, the Persians were soon menacing Athens. Fearing the worst, the Athenians evacuated the city and moved their outnumbered fleet to an anchorage off Salamis, a nearby island in the Saronic Gulf. Confident of triumph, King Xerxes had his throne set up on the beach so he could watch as his warships pursued the Athenians into the narrow straits between the island and mainland, but the ensuing battle could not have been to his liking. Far from winning, the Persian navy was put to flight. Worse, a sizable land force left behind for the winter met a similar fate at Plataea, about 30 miles northwest of Athens, the following year.

Though deliverance was sweet, the Athenians' celebrations were no doubt tempered with sadness, for the invaders left in Athens a scene of utter devastation. "Of the encircling wall only small portions were left standing," reports the historian Thucydides, "and most of the houses were in ruins, only a few remaining in which the chief men of the Persians had themselves taken quarters." On the Acropolis, Athenians found their temples, shrines, and sacred statues broken and defiled. Vowing never to rebuild these, but to leave them in ruins "as a memorial to those who come after of the impiety of the barbarians," Athenians reverently buried the debris *(pages 34-35).*

Among the pieces disposed of in this way were 14 beautifully carved marble maidens, or *korai,* found by excavators of the Greek Archaeological Society in 1886. Dating to the late sixth century BC, the figures had obviously been laid in the ground with care, for the archaeologists discovered them lying side by side, as if sleeping. Their elaborately crinkled hairstyles and folded garments had lost none of their crisp clarity after some 2,300 years in the soil, and green, dark red, and gold paint still clung to the edges of the gowns.

Themistocles was quick to mobilize his fellow citizens to rebuild other parts of the city. In 479 BC, for instance, they built a massive wall around all of Athens. Remains of the venture have been uncovered at the Dipylon, or main city gate, located northwest of the Agora. Though the ramparts were hastily thrown together from

Found in the Agora with six bronze ballots still inside, this terra-cotta ballot box was used by Athenian juries to render verdicts. As shown in the details at top, the ballots had short axles, some hollow and some solid. Casting a hollow ballot signified a guilty vote; a solid ballot was a vote in favor of the defendant.

whatever stone lay to hand, including even funeral monuments, they were broad enough "for two trains of wagons to cross one another as they brought up the stones," Thucydides wrote—more than enough to have presented a formidable obstacle to any aggressor. Later, toward the middle of the century, two parallel walls were built to connect the Themistoclean walls with similar ramparts encircling Piraeus, Athens's port, five and a half miles away.

That the Long Walls, as the pair were called, attached the city to Piraeus, Athens's outlet to the sea, was as significant as their defensive capabilities, for after Salamis, Athens emerged as the Greek world's preeminent maritime power. In addition to ensuring unprecedented prosperity, the position brought a number of political consequences, but none so important as defending against future aggression. To this end, Athens and a number of other Greek city-states in 477 BC formed an alliance against Persia called the Delian League after the Aegean island of Delos, where its treasury was located. Given the option of providing either ships or money, most league members contributed money, only to watch their donations make the Athenians— whose triremes gave the confederation its backbone—richer and stronger while the Persian threat faded away. By 454 BC, when the league treasury was transferred to Athens, the alliance had come to resemble an empire.

More than 100 fragments of inscribed stone unearthed on the Acropolis give an idea of the wealth that was pouring into the city at that time. Fitted together by a pair of American scholars in 1927, the pieces formed a series of marble slabs, or steles, on which were carved the accounts of the treasurers of Athena for 454 to 414 BC, recording their share (one-sixtieth) of the sum paid by league members in return for Athens's protection. The ledgers show that as many as 265 cities paid tribute, the amount of their contribution calculated on the basis of cultivable land or commercial prosperity, but that only 50 to 65 percent of the cities paid in any one year.

The man who led Athens at this time of plenty was Pericles,

a young nobleman and Assembly member whose power and influence extended far beyond the limits of his elected position. Under him, the democratic reforms of his great-uncle Cleisthenes reached their fullest expression: Economic barriers to holding public office were dashed, and for the first time, citizens who performed public service received compensation for it. No longer would an artisan or a laborer have to suffer a reduction in income for time spent as a juror or a member of the boule. But it is Pericles' wide-ranging program of public building, and the controversial way that he paid for it, for which he is best remembered.

Brushing aside charges that the city's political life had become "democracy in name, but in practice government by the first citizen," as well as complaints that the Athenians were boldly abusing their office as treasurers to the league, Pericles used Delian League money to erect court buildings, colonnaded marketplaces, theaters, and gymnasiums in and around Athens. He placed the famed sculptor Phidias in overall charge of construction. Then, abandoning the Athenians' earlier vow to leave the ruined Acropolis as it was, Pericles hired the greatest architects of the age to transform it into a gleaming wonder of the world.

A monumental gateway was erected to replace a simpler archaic entrance, portions of which have been unearthed by archaeologists, at the hilltop's western end. Called the Propylaea, the Periclean structure enclosed an inclined central chariot road, flanking column-lined porches, and a main gate about 25 feet high and nearly 14 feet wide. Overhead, recalled the second-century AD traveler Pausanias, a coffered marble ceiling sparkled with gold stars on a blue background. "Such magnificence in a secular building," wrote Demosthenes, "was a splendid extravagance."

About 130 feet east of the Propylaea and almost aligned with its central passageway stood a monumental bronze Athena that Phidias created

These ostraca, or potsherds, were used by Athenians to vote for ostracism—the 10-year exile of leaders whose rising power made them potential dictators. When citizens gathered for such a vote, each of them carried a pottery fragment etched with the name of the person he wanted to banish. The ostracon on the left was aimed at the statesman Pericles; the one at right bears the name Thucydides, possibly the grandfather of the great historian of the same name.

between 465 and 455 BC to commemorate the Athenians' victory at Marathon. Sadly, the figure—known as Athena Promachos, or Athena the Champion—was apparently removed to Constantinople, where it perished, so scholars know little about it other than that it rested on a podium, fragments of which still survive, and that Athena wore a helmet and held a shield and a spear. According to Pausanias, the statue of Athena stood so tall that sailors aboard ships off Sounion, a promontory located at the southernmost tip of Attica, about 37 miles from Athens, could make out the crest of the goddess's helmet and the point of her spear.

Another 160 feet to the east of the statue, on the sacred spot where the ruler of Mycenaean Athens had his palace seven centuries earlier, Pericles planned construction of an elegant shrine called the Erechtheum. Designed to accommodate altars of Zeus, Poseidon, and the smith god Hephaestus, as well as house the ancient wooden cult statue of Athena, the temple incorporated a number of architectural curiosities, including two distinctive porches at its west end.

Square openings in the ceiling and floor of the northern porch marked a spot said to have been

A MODERN TRIREME PUTS TO SEA

Like a ghost ship, or something out of a time machine, a strange vessel began appearing in waters south of Athens in the late 1980s (right). In fact, the craft was a modern replica of an ancient Greek galley, or trireme—so called

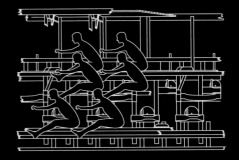

because of its three banks of oars.

Swift, nimble, and deadly, these sleek vessels had defended democratic Athens for generations. But no detailed descriptions of a trireme exist, and archaeologists have never found remains of one of the ships. For centuries, historians could only surmise—

from fragmentary contemporary records and depictions on coins, carvings, and vase paintings—how the craft were actually constructed and propelled. Much of the uncertainty centered on the placement of the oarsmen and the relative lengths of their oars.

In 1982 three Britishers—

struck by Poseidon's trident, and six beautifully carved marble maidens called caryatids were used as columns for the roof of the southern porch. Though the figures vary in the folds of their gowns and in their stances—three rest on their right leg, while the others stand on their left—all face south, toward Pericles' crowning jewel: the magnificent columned shrine of Athena. Callicrates, overseer of construction of the Long Walls, and Ictinus, designer of the Temple of Apollo at Bassae, erected this shrine above the south face of the Acropolis.

At the heart of the temple stood a rectangular central structure, or cella, that was divided into two rooms. The name of the west chamber—the Parthenon, or room of the maidens—would be applied to the entire temple as early as the fourth century. It is thought that the west room was intended as the residence of the few mortals who were privileged to serve the gods, but it later took on more worldly purpose: treasury for the Athenian empire.

The east chamber, the larger of the two, housed another statue of Athena by Phidias, this one 39 feet tall and made of wood, gold, and ivory. Like the bronze Athena, this figure too was carried off to Constantinople and lost. Yet scholars know from representations on ancient coins, Roman copies, and Pausanias that Phidias depicted the

writer Frank Welsh, classical scholar John Morrison, and naval architect John Coates—organized the Trireme Trust, with the goal of building and sailing one of the legendary vessels. One of their first steps was to test a mock-up of the warship's oar system, which they determined employed oars of equal length and oarsmen positioned as shown in the drawing at far left. After demonstrating its model, the trust received from the Greek government a commitment to finance a complete trireme.

Construction began in 1985 at a boatyard near the port of Piraeus. As much as possible, the builders used the techniques and materials of ancient shipwrights, in-

cluding 17,000 handmade iron nails and 22,000 oak dowels. Their pine planking, however, came from Oregon—Mediterranean pines no longer grow tall or straight enough for sheathing ships' hulls. And while the ancients helped hold their triremes together with a stem-to-stern pair of flax ropes, the modern builders opted for sturdier polymer ropes.

The completed vessel—121

feet long and 20 feet wide—got its first sea trials in 1987 and in 1988 was christened the *Olympias* and commissioned in the Greek navy. Subsequent speed trials have shown that with all 170 rowers bending to their oars, the craft can cruise at about 5½ knots. Top speed—at which the ancients would have employed the vessel's deadly, bronze-tipped ram (*below*)—is about 10 knots.

To mark the 2,500th anniversary of Athenian democracy, the *Olympias* made a symbolic voyage on the Thames at London in 1993. Its mission: to deliver a copy of an ancient decree for the defense of democracy, a cause that the old triremes had served so well.

goddess as a helmeted warrior and set a coiled serpent beside her as a symbol of her power. He placed a shield and a spear in her left hand and a six-foot-tall winged figure of Nike, goddess of victory, in her right.

A 525-foot continuous frieze depicting the Panathenaic procession ran around the outside of the cella walls. Starting above a narrow columned porch at the structure's west end, more than 200 marchers—horsemen, charioteers, musicians, city elders, pitcher bearers, sacrificial animals—were presented in low relief. Moving eastward across the north and south sides, they came into the company of the gods over another porch at the far end, a mirror image of the one in the west.

Forty-six columns—each more than six feet in diameter at its base and more than 32 feet tall—ringed the temple, supporting its pitched roof but also making it difficult for visitors standing outside the Parthenon to view the cella frieze. Above them rested another frieze, this one showing battle scenes in which gods are pitted against giants and Greeks fight centaurs and other mythological figures. The images were carved in high relief on 92 marble metopes set apart from one another by triglyphs, stone slabs adorned with three vertical grooves.

Some 50 marble sculptures were positioned above the metopes in the triangular gables, or pediments, at the temple's front and back. According to Pausanias, the birth of Athena was depicted in the east, while she and Poseidon, lord of the seas, were shown struggling for control of Athens in the west. On evidence of such shrines as the Temple of Zeus at Olympia, historians know that ancient sculptors rarely spent much time finishing the backside of such pedimental sculpture, which viewers on the ground could not see. Yet the artists who chiseled the Parthenon figures—perhaps believing that their work was going to be visible to gods on high—carved them as if they were to be displayed at ground level.

More amazing, according to Plutarch, was the speed with which the principal Acropolis buildings were erected. "Each one of them, men thought, would require many successive generations to complete it," he wrote, "but all of them were fully completed in the heyday of a single administration." Annual accounts kept by the citizen commission that oversaw expenditures for the project reflect this. Inscribed on stone

Shown below in a Turkish manuscript, this gilded-bronze monument of three serpents was raised at Delphi in the fifth century BC to mark a Greek victory over the Persians at Plataea in 479 BC. The column was seized in the fourth century AD and taken to Constantinople (Istanbul) where part of it still stands (left) *as a fountain. A portion of one serpent's head* (above) *is in an Istanbul museum.*

slabs, fragments of which have been recovered, the accounts reveal that payments for quarrying marble at Mount Pentelicus, about 10 miles to the northwest, and transporting it to the Acropolis began in 447 BC. The Parthenon's columns are mentioned in the accounts for 441 BC, implying that construction of the colonnade was already under way. Only three years later, in 438 BC, the Athenians dedicated Phidias's ivory and gold image of the maiden. At that time, scholars say, Athena had to have a roof over her head, and the cella frieze and metopes must have been not only carved but also installed.

Similar inscriptions found on the Acropolis during the 18th and 19th centuries demonstrate that many laborers were required to get so much work done in so little time. Besides noting expenses incurred during the construction of the Erechtheum in 409 BC—for animal sacrifices and for gold leaf, lead, struts, gutters, and other items—the accounts list a wide array of artisans, including carpenters, stonemasons, gilders, painters, carriers of paint pots, block and tackle operators, and sculptors. Citizens, resident aliens, and slaves worked side by side and earned equal pay for equal work. With wages for skilled labor running at a drachma a day, a sculptor could expect to be paid only 60 drachmas for the two months of carving required to produce a single small figure.

Variations in styles of carving, especially in the Parthenon frieze, also betray the number of sculptors hired to work on the Acropolis under Phidias's watchful eye. While one rendered horses with close-cut, bushy manes, another gave his steeds long, individually carved hairs that waved in the wind. Figures elsewhere on the shrine bear scars of the project's hurried pace. In the west pediment, for example, a sculptor seems to have miscalculated the space available for the head of a horse. To make the piece fit during installation, a mason apparently cut chunks of marble from the top of its head and the side of its jaw. Workers performed similar emergency surgery while mounting a beautifully executed but ill-fitting seated female figure thought to be the goddess Hestia.

97

Such minor flaws, however, do not detract from the breathtaking degree of technical precision achieved by the builders, as a host of 19th-century visitors attested. Among them was a 28-year-old British architect, surveyor, and antiquary named Francis Cranmer Penrose, who in 1845 made the first accurate measurements of the Parthenon. Among the many marvels he revealed was that the stylobate, the rectangular masonry platform underlying the temple's colonnade, was not flat but gently arched. Its midpoint lay exactly 228 millimeters—or a thousandth of its length—higher than its corners. The curvature, in the estimation of one scholar, was meant "to impart a feeling of life and to prevent the appearance of sagging."

Penrose also scrutinized the Parthenon's columns, which did not stand perpendicular but leaned slightly inward. Noting this 20 centuries earlier, the famed Roman engineer and architect Vitruvius observed that the inclination contributed to the temple's imposing, rock-solid appearance. Yet until Penrose, no one could have imagined how subtly the effect had been achieved, for the columns leaned no more than two and three-eighths of an inch away from vertical—meaning that if their axes were projected skyward, they would meet a mile and a half above the surface of the earth.

The contour of the columns was equally sophisticated. Evidently concerned that pencil-straight, cylindrical columns might appear concave when viewed from a distance, the stonecutters made them slightly cigar shaped. Widest at the base, the shafts dramatically decrease in diameter two-fifths of the way up, Penrose found. Such attention to detail reflects the high skill of the Parthenon's builders, because they worked with only the simplest of tools—cords, plumb lines, water levels, squares, and perhaps a long, flexible wooden ruler.

The builders' bold, imaginative refashioning of the Acropolis reflected the full glory of Periclean Athens—its wealth and might, its elegance and sophistication, its pride and collective determination. And in the years to come, people from all across the Greek world dedicated altars and idols there—so many, in fact, that the Acropolis soon resembled what one scholar has described as a "close-packed, largely open-air museum of art, piety and history."

Just southeast of the Propylaea, for instance, stood a 126-foot-long colonnaded structure that housed a statue of the fertility goddess Artemis by the famed sculptor Praxiteles. Nearby, according to ancient accounts, was a bronze Trojan Horse complete with tiny Greeks peering from its inside. And according to Pausanias, two

Painted by 19th-century French artist Alexis Paccard, this watercolor re-creates a corner of the Parthenon as it might have looked in its heyday. But Paccard failed to convey the intensity of the original colors, which would have made the ornamentation stand out at a distance.

additional figures shaded a rock-cut road stretching from the Erechtheum to the Propylaea: one of them was of Pericles himself, and a second was yet another bronze Athena by Phidias, commissioned by settlers of the Aegean island of Lemnos, that Pausanias regarded as "the best worth seeing" of the artist's works.

Sadly, all that remains of these statues are the bases, some in fragments, that once supported them and cuttings in the rocky Acropolis floor. Converted into a Christian church in the late sixth century AD, then reconfigured as a mosque and a stronghold by the Turks and bombarded by the Venetians, Athena's temple stood defaced and shattered when in September of 1834 an international group of antiquaries, led by Bavarian architect Leo von Klenze, made the first attempt to return the Acropolis to its Periclean glory.

Heinrich Schliemann, the discoverer of Troy, numbered among the many restorers who followed in von Klenze's footsteps. In 1875 he financed the demolition of a 70-foot-high stone tower, erected on the site of the Propylaea in the Middle Ages, that he felt was "marring the harmonious lines of the entire Acropolis." But it was not until Nikolaos Balanos, a Greek civil engineer, began work around the turn of the century that the Acropolis took on the appearance familiar around the world today.

Hoping to restore to the ruins a "part of their former grandeur," Balanos rebuilt portions of the Erechtheum and Propylaea, including part of the gateway's coffered marble ceiling, before turning his attention in 1923 to reerecting the Parthenon's north and south colonnades. Searching the Acropolis for the marble drums that originally made up the columns, Balanos

GIVING THE PAST A FUTURE

It took the ancient Greeks about 15 years to complete the Parthenon, the great temple that crowns the Acropolis of Athens *(far right)*. It will take considerably longer to complete the current project to reinforce and restore this magnificent structure.

The ambitious undertaking grew out of a 1971 UNESCO report warning that the effects of time, earlier salvage efforts, and modern-day air pollution threatened the Parthenon and three neighboring buildings—the Erechtheum, the Propylaea, and the Temple of Athena Nike—with collapse. Four years later, the Greek government formed the Committee for the Preservation of the Acropolis Monuments to oversee efforts to save these world treasures.

Key among those working on the project is architect Manolis Korres *(above, right)*, who is now supervising restoration of the Parthenon. Earlier, he had helped in the preservation of the Erechtheum, whose renowned caryatids—pillars in the form of graceful females—had been all but obliterated by acid rain and other pollutants. Replaced by concrete replicas, the originals (except for one in London, removed by Lord Elgin) are now in the Acropolis Museum.

Korres, a native Athenian who has been captivated by the

Parthenon since childhood, brings to his task an unmatched enthusiasm and knowledge. "He knows that building," Brian F. Cook, keeper of Greek and Roman antiquities at the British Museum, has said. "He knows every stone in a way that no man alive and probably no man dead has ever known it."

Indeed, Korres and his associates have painstakingly combed through the tens of thousands of stone fragments littering the Acropolis and managed to find close to a thousand that came originally from the Parthenon itself. Simply by observing the texture, color, chisel markings, and patterns of wear on a stray chunk of marble, Korres not only can often tell that the piece belongs to the Parthenon but can also determine exactly where it fits into the ancient structure.

Whenever possible, these stray pieces are placed in their

original spots, and Korres strives to use as little new material as possible. Even when fresh marble is employed to complete a broken block, the architect says, "we do it in such a way that if in the future the original fragment is found, someone can remove the new marble and attach the original fragment."

The preservation committee, made up of architects, archaeologists, civil engineers, and chemists, has no intention of returning the Parthenon to its fifth-century BC condition. Rather, the goal is to stabilize and preserve it as a ruin that has for so long stood as a cherished icon of Western culture. Every alteration of that familiar configuration—no matter how slight—must go through a rigorous review process that reaches all the way up to the Greek Ministry of Culture.

Not everyone fully approves of the committee's plans. Most controversial, perhaps, is Korres' scheme to include in the restoration some traces of the alterations made to the Parthenon over the centuries. For example, he intends to show parts of the Muslim mosque that was erected inside the temple soon after the Ottoman conquest. Some critics maintain that preservation efforts should be aimed only at the original building.

For all that, much of Korres'

Counterweighted by huge blocks of concrete, this French-built crane is used to hoist the Parthenon's heavy slabs and drums. When not in operation, the cream-colored crane can be folded into itself so that it does not intrude on the view of the Acropolis.

efforts so far have been directed at removing and replacing the corroded iron clamps and reinforcing rods installed in the Parthenon by Greek civil engineer Nikolaos Balanos earlier in this century. And when he has finished replacing scattered parts and rebuilding walls and columns—sometime early in the 21st century—the building will be only about 10 percent more complete than when he began.

A restorer atop the southwest corner of the Parthenon holds one of the modern clamps being used to join the temple's marble blocks. Like the dowel lying to his left, the bracket was specially made of titanium to keep it from rusting. The Parthenon's east doorway and the partially reconstructed cella walls are visible in the background.

Below, stonemasons trained in ancient carving techniques try to fit two marble pieces. To qualify as a match, the contour of the fragments, the color, veining, and brittleness of the marble, and any chisel marks must all be similar.

Above, fragments that Korres has identified as belonging to the Parthenon await cataloging. Culled from the thousands of stones that litter the Acropolis, such pieces are like lost words of an "important but as yet fragmentary text," Korres says.

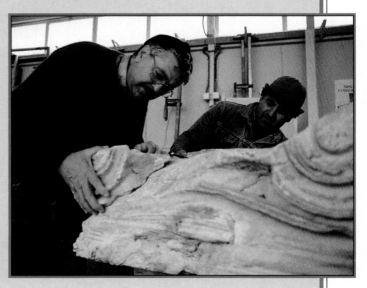

found that the builders of the Parthenon had marked each piece with a combination of red letters and slashes. The letters, he discovered, indicated to which column a particular drum belonged, while the slashes showed the order in which the pieces were to be stacked. The markings also made clear which drums were missing. For these, Balanos made replacements from concrete, since the material was thought to blend more harmoniously with ancient stone than fresh, unweathered marble. Once the columns were reconstructed, Balanos reversed the capitals that rested upon them, turning the pieces through 180 degrees so that their cleaner, less exposed sides would face outward. Atop these he set new architrave blocks fashioned from marble quarried at times from the same sources used by Pericles' builders. He used thousands of discreetly placed iron pins and clamps to help hold the sections together.

Thanks to Balanos, by 1933 the Parthenon had been returned, as much as had then been possible, to the way it was thought to have appeared almost 250 years before, yet scholars remain divided as to how far this achievement is to be applauded. As early as 1922 Balanos's own assistant, Anastasios Orlandos, objected to reerecting the temple's north colonnade without also restoring the cella walls and publicly broke with his master. And others have charged that Balanos, in his eagerness to build an impressive testimonial to the glory of Periclean Athens, showed insufficient respect for what was known of the temple's actual form.

Balanos did use whatever marble lay to hand in his reconstruction, sometimes paying too little attention to where each piece originally belonged. Worse, when a stone was inconveniently

Based on the excavations that got under way in 1931, this scale model (right) recreates the Agora and its public buildings as they looked in about 400 BC. The landmark Hephaisteion stands on the hillside at far left. Below and to the left is the circular Tholos, where representatives of Athens's 10 tribes rotated duty to ensure that emergencies and the day-to-day business of the city would be taken care of around the clock. At the far right lower corner is the red-roofed mint.

shaped, he recut it so that it fit where he wanted it to go. Most damaging of all, the iron pins he used have oxidized and expanded, cracking apart the blocks they were intended to bind. Balanos knew this might happen but went ahead—leaving to modern restorers the daunting task of putting his wrongs to right *(pages 100-103)*.

Unlike those who have worked on the Acropolis, the archaeologists entrusted with the excavation of the Agora—the main marketplace and civic center of classical Athens—have escaped such controversy, if only because the site proved so difficult to find. Built over time and again since the Middle Ages, its exact location long forgotten amid the noise and grime of the modern city, the Agora lay undisturbed until 1929, when the American School of Classical Studies, financed by American millionaire John D. Rockefeller Jr., became determined to find it.

For as long as anyone could remember, an excellently preserved fifth-century marble temple, known once as the Theseum but now as the Hephaisteion, had commanded a hill to the west of the area assumed to be the Agora. And as early as 1859 the Greek Archaeological Society had cleared the Stoa of Attalos, a large marble and limestone colonnaded building erected along the east side of the square in the second century BC. Yet it was not until 1934, when the Americans uncovered the remains of a simple, circular building more than 60 feet in diameter, that the Agora could be identified with certainty, for here they recognized the heart of fifth-century BC

Athenian democracy—the Tholos. Inside its walls, ancient sources tell, were fed the 50 members of the *prytaneis,* or executive committee. Drawn on a rotating basis from the body of 500 that formed the boule of Cleisthenes, they were responsible for the day-to-day governance of Athens, and no fewer than 17 of their number resided in the Tholos around the clock, so they would be ever ready to deal with emergencies. Fragments of the black-glazed ceramic bowls, cups, and jugs from which they took their meals—evidence of the committee members' steadfast vigilance—were uncovered by the archaeologists.

The pieces represent a mere fraction of the thousands of pottery sherds that have been dug up in the Agora since then. Together with almost 700 references to the site in ancient texts and some 7,500 inscriptions—many of which begin with the day, month, and year of their carving, the year given by the name of the chief magistrate at the time—they have enabled archaeologists not only to trace the physical outlines of the marketplace but also to compile a detailed chronology for it.

Such evidence shows that in preclassical times the Agora lay outside the city and was used as a burial ground. In fact, the tract did not take on the character of a civic center until the early sixth century, when Solon's reforms made necessary a space for public meetings and Pisistratus's reorganization of the Panathenaea gave new importance to the Panathenaic Way, the ancient thoroughfare that crossed the site from the northwest to the southeast and led to the Acropolis.

After Cleisthenes instituted his reforms in the late sixth century BC, his popular Assembly gathered by the thousands in a semicircular, theater-like seating space on the slope of a hill some 1,300 feet to the southwest of the Agora. But foundation remains indicate that the boule met in a square-shaped building that was located just north of the Tholos. Though evidence for the date of the structure is slight, most experts agree that it was built around 500 BC and

Thought to be the foundations of the shop owned by the shoemaker Simon, a friend of Socrates', these ruins were unearthed on the fringes of the Agora. The shop's clay floor was littered with iron hobnails (inset, above) *used to stud the soles of heavy-duty sandals.*

remained in use until about 415 to 406 BC. Then, for reasons that remain unknown, the council was moved to a new structure located just to the west and the old one was converted into the city's official archives and renamed the Metroon.

By then, asserts John Camp, the director of the American school's excavations, the Agora was well established as the hub around which classical Athens turned. "Within the great open square, monuments were set up to commemorate her triumphs," he says of Athens. "Along its edges were the civic buildings for the administration of her democracy, while beyond its borders crowded the houses and workshops of those who made Athens the foremost city of Greece." Among these is a row of fifth-century buildings discovered along a street leading from the southeast corner of the Agora. Located in a busy commercial area, the structures housed shops, workshops, and at least one thriving tavern, as the contents of a nearby well made clear. In addition to animal bones, mussel shells, and other rubbish, it held cooking pots and tableware, drinking cups, and a number of amphorae imported from all over the classical world.

Excavators have revealed that the southeast corner was also home to the city's mint. Within the foundations of a fifth-century building they uncovered the remains of items used for heating and then cooling precious metals—furnaces and cement-lined water basins—and 10 small bronze disks. Thought to be the blanks for coins, they needed only to be stamped before they could be issued as currency and carried to the farthest corners of the Greek world.

Some 240 of the coins were found in the remains of a double-colonnaded building located not far from the mint along the south side of the Agora's open area. Built between 430 and 420 BC and stretching more than 260 feet from east to west, the stoa fronted a row of 16 square rooms, each of which was entered through a door cut in its north wall. Because the entryways were located not centrally but about a foot east of the midpoint, archaeologists figure the chambers may have been designed to accommodate dining couches. They were likely set head to foot flush against the interior walls, so that pairs of jurors or other officials could have dined along the east, south, and west walls, while thanks to the offset doorway, a seventh could have been served along the north.

Open to the air but shielded from rain and the worst of the afternoon sun, a number of similar stoas stood around the Agora's perimeter. The most famous of these, a limestone and marble building 41 feet wide and at least 118 feet long, occupied a prime spot near the square's northwest corner. From its broad, southeast-facing colonnade, ancient Greeks could have taken in the entire Agora at a glance and let their gaze follow the Panathenaic Way to the Acropolis looming in the distance.

The structure took its name—Stoa Poikilê, or Painted Stoa—from a series of large paintings that, according to Pausanias and other sources, adorned its walls for some six centuries. Created by the greatest painters of the age—including Polygnotus, whose works were also displayed in a picture gallery located in the Propylaea—the murals depicted the Greeks at Troy, the Athenians at Marathon, and other great scenes, mythological as well as historic, and were complemented by a display of military memorabilia commemorating the city's triumphs in war.

The trophies have almost all disappeared, but they are known to have included a number of shields taken from vanquished Spartan warriors. One of these, a bronze weapon about a yard in diameter adorned with a decorative border, was found in a cistern that excavators say was filled up in the third century BC. Though the metal was badly corroded and its leather lining was completely missing, the shield was still recognizable, thanks to an inscription punched across the front, proudly confirming its capture in 425 BC in an early battle of the Peloponnesian War.

Against this background of war scenes and booty, Athenians pursued such peaceful occupations as crafting deals and discussing politics, shopping, or watching the jugglers, sword swallowers, and other entertainers who came to amuse them. The large crowds drew antiquity's great thinkers as well—including the philosopher Zeno, who arrived in Athens from his native Cyprus around 300 BC. His followers, the Stoics, met so frequently at the Painted Stoa that they took its name as their own.

Ancient sources say Socrates too was a familiar sight in the Agora, perched in whatever convenient spot he could find with a knot of students around him. But when he had to teach students too young to enter the Agora proper—an area reserved for adult men—Xenophon, one of his disciples, says the philosopher held class in a cobbler's shop belonging to a friend named Simon. Although identifying ancient structures is always difficult, archaeologists digging southwest of the Agora uncovered the remains of a fifth-century shop that seems to match the historian's description *(page 106)*. A large

Silhouetted by the setting sun, the columns of the ruined Temple of Poseidon rise above the Aegean Sea at Sunium, on the southernmost tip of the Attic coast. Erected during the age of Pericles, the shrine has served for centuries as a marker for mariners.

quantity of iron hobnails and bone rings—used as eyelets for laces—was found on its floor, and a black-glazed drinking cup inscribed with the name Simon was unearthed on the street outside.

Socrates, born only 20 years after the battle of Marathon, was 16 years old when the Delian League treasury was transferred to Athens, 35 when work began on the Erechtheum, and 66 when Athens—having suffered a devastating defeat at Syracuse, in Sicily, and faced with turmoil and revolution at home—finally capitulated to the Spartans in 404 BC. Five years later, the great philosopher would be dead. Convicted of corrupting the minds of Athenian youth through his teachings, Socrates was forced to commit suicide by drinking hemlock. Plato, his most distinguished student, left Athens in disgust, only to return later and found his own school of philosophy, known as the Academy, on a wooded spot northwest of the city.

The site had long been home to both a shrine sacred to Athena and an archaic gymnasium, or sporting grounds, frequented by young Athenian men, who came to exercise, pass the time in discussion, and socialize. There Plato practiced the teaching methods of his mentor, as a comic dialogue of the time makes clear. Asked what Plato was up to, a character remarks, "I saw a crowd of young men in the gymnasia of the Academy, earnestly trying to define whether a pumpkin is a vegetable, a grass, or a tree, while Plato stood benevolently by encouraging them."

Efforts mounted in the 1930s and again in the years after World War II have revealed only a few tantalizing physical details of

Plato's Academy. In addition to a number of structures dating to Roman imperial times, a sixth-century marble boundary stone almost three feet tall has been found, marking out one limit of the precinct, along with a nearby row of large column bases thought to be the remains of a colonnaded court. Archaeologists consider it likely that the columns, which have been dated to the fourth century BC, may once have shaded Plato himself.

When Plato died in 348 BC, the heyday of the Academy had already passed. Gone too were the years when the independent states that made up the Greek world were able to unite against a common enemy, as they had once done against Persia. In most cities, small cliques of wealthy men clashed with democrats, and almost everywhere tyrants had reappeared. Democracy faltered in Athens as well, as it fell prey to worsening financial difficulties and politicians devoted more of their energies to savage personal attacks than to the issues of the day. Lawsuits proliferated. In fact, Athenians sued one another so regularly that the famed orator Demosthenes, the orphaned son of a proprietor of a sword and cutlery factory, started his career writing, and sometimes delivering, speeches for private litigants. About half of the 61 addresses that scholars say he wrote dealt with private, rather than political, topics. Yet Demosthenes is most famous for his political oratory, especially for a series of speeches given between 352 and 340 BC in which he urged his fellow Greeks to join together against a new and powerful menace—Philip II, the recently crowned king of Macedon. Demosthenes, history records, argued passionately, eloquently, and as it turned out, correctly, but his words fell upon deaf ears. ▧

TREASURES FROM THE DEEP

Many of the monumental Greek bronze sculptures that exist today have been retrieved—through incredible luck—from the bottom of the Mediterranean. Together with a few other survivors excavated on land, they represent but a small percentage of the hundreds, if not thousands, of such large bronzes that once stood in Greek cities and sanctuaries. Precisely how these superb statues came to languish in the muck and sand remains unknown. Most were probably removed from their pedestals by Romans, after their conquest of Greece in the second century BC, for shipment to Italy, there to decorate the gardens of the wealthy in love with a culture they deemed more refined than their own. But not all ships made it; some sank during storms, taking their cargoes with them. Several of the rescued figures have been discovered near the decayed timbers of Roman vessels or along coastal routes used by Roman navigators. The magnificent head above, thought to be that of a Greek philosopher, was recovered in 1969 in the Strait of Messina, between Italy and Sicily.

The first underwater finds of monumental bronzes were made during the early 1900s by Greek sponge divers. After their long submersion, the corroded, encrusted, and often fragmented statues required immediate care. To preserve these and later discoveries, scientists have since refined painstaking methods of cleaning and restoring the figures, resorting to a variety of high-tech tools and equipment to aid them in their delicate task. In recent decades, too, archaeologists using Aqua-Lungs and other advanced gear have been able to dive to ever greater depths and to methodically examine wrecks on the Mediterranean floor, in hopes not only of learning more about the early maritime world but also of finding additional sculptures.

nchored off the coast of the island of Antikythera in October 1900, the crew of a fishing vessel was looking for sponges when one of the men, near panic, bobbed to the surface in his diving suit and began babbling about the things he had seen below. "A heap of dead naked women," he said, were mixed on the bottom with piles of other "green corpses." The captain donned the suit and went to investigate. Soon he was back, with a corroded bronze arm attached to his lifeline.

So began the first great discovery of full-size Greek bronze statuary in the sea. Returning the next month to the watery site between Crete and the Greek mainland with a navy ship and archaeologists, the divers brought up from 180 feet pieces of the magnificent statue at right, along with portions of several lesser figures, all cargo of a Roman ship that sank around 80 BC.

The next epochal find was in 1925, when fishermen trawling the bay off the ancient battle site of Marathon snagged a net on the bronze of the nude youth at left. Then, in 1928, sponge divers made an even greater find near Cape Artemisium in the Aegean—heroic figures of a god, a boy, and a horse (overleaf). And in 1972 two other life-size bronze statues (last four pages of this essay) were discovered off southern Italy to dazzle modern eyes with their fierce beauty.

Dreamy in expression, the so-called Marathon Boy, seen at left in closeup, gazes downward, his eyes focused on an object he held in his left hand that is now missing. The hornlike protuberance on his curly head is part of a circlet. The four-foot, three-inch-tall sculpture was probably cast, like the figure at right, during the late fourth century BC.

With his head turned away from his weight-bearing leg, the magnificently balanced six-foot, four-inch-tall bronze of a young man at right existed only in fragments when found by sponge divers working off the Greek island of Antikythera in 1900. Reassembled soon afterward, it underwent a second, more thorough restoration in the 1950s.

One of the masterpieces rescued from 140 feet of water off Cape Artemisium, this almost seven-foot-tall figure of a god—thought to be Zeus about to hurl a thunderbolt—radiates ferocious energy as well as divine nobility. The statue's dramatic design, with the arms stretching full length from the torso and making the figure slightly wider than it is tall, was only possible for sculptors using bronze rather than marble.

A youthful jockey—also found off Cape Artemisium—clings with his legs to the back of an eight-foot-long, galloping racehorse. Divers working at the site failed to find some parts of the horse; restorers have supplied sections of the body, a hoof, and the overly tame tail. A small segment of the jockey's tunic preserved on the horse's mane proves that the boy, discovered some distance from his steed, was in fact intended to be its rider.

Stefano Mariottini, a chemist from Rome, was snorkeling some 300 yards off the southern coast of Italy at Riace Marina on the last day of his vacation in the summer of 1972 when he saw "something black"—he thought it was part of a human corpse—sticking up from the sandy bottom. Swimming nearer on a second dive, he touched the object and found it to be metal, not flesh. Then, on a third foray, Mariottini brushed some sand aside and uncovered, to his astonishment, two statues.

Lifted from the sand by trained divers *(below)* and borne to the surface with the aid of polyethylene balloons filled with compressed air,

the corroded and encrusted figures turned out to be the pair of magnificent Greek statues—soon dubbed Warrior A and Warrior B—shown on the next pages.

Taken to the museum in the nearby city of Reggio, the warriors underwent two years of cleaning, before being moved to Florence for an additional five years' work. Not only did layer after layer of encrusted sand, gravel, and marine life have to be painstakingly removed; the statues' corroded metal itself required attention, inside as well as out. The statues' clay cores, used by the Greek sculptors when pouring the molten metal, had absorbed quantities of lime and sea salts and

now were exuding chlorides that were eating away at the bronze. This required a delicate operation to flush out most of the clay.

After extensive restoration in Florence, the statues were finally returned to the small but proud museum in Reggio that had laid claim to the stupendous visitors from the sea. There, following some 10 years on display, the figures began to show signs of deterioration. Acting quickly, experts *(right)* undertook the challenge of extracting the remaining clay, beginning with Warrior B. Hopefully, when work on both of the statues is complete, the Riace bronzes will survive for yet another 2,000 years.

Divers guide the statue of Warrior A (above, left) *as it is lifted from the seabed in 1972. Each of the figures weighs about 1,000 pounds. Because of this, they may have been heaved overboard to lighten a foundering vessel during a storm. But 28 lead rings, perhaps from the rigging, found on the seabed suggest that the ship may have sunk after all.*

Covered with the mineral and barnacle encrustations that were produced by 2,000 years in sea and sand, the back of Warrior B before cleaning appears to be afflicted with a skin disease. The restorers in Florence labored to remove the detritus from both warriors using a variety of delicate tools, including scalpels, small pneumatic drills, ultrasonic picks, and microsanders.

A team of specialists works on Warrior B in a partitioned section of the Reggio museum where the sculptures are housed. Restorer Mario Micheli (far right) inserts a probe, which is normally used for endoscopic surgery in humans, into an opening in the right foot of the statue. Equipped with a tiny camera, the probe can reach even into knees and elbows and transmit images of the interior onto a television monitor. The restorers can then direct ultrasonic waves at trouble spots and loosen remnants of the ancient clay core for final removal.

Grotesque horns protrude from the eyes and mouth of Warrior B after the restorers in Florence, making a first attempt to wash the clay core and other debris from inside the statue, injected peroxide and ammonia solutions. The mixture of chemicals, clay, and sand frothed from the warrior's orifices and then hardened.

Almost frightening in their massive power—"you could not live with it in your room," said one scholar of Warrior A—the over six-foot-tall bronzes rescued near Reggio remain astonishingly intact despite 20 centuries in the sea. They lack only the shields and weapons they once carried, the helmet Warrior B (far right) doubtless wore, and a few other details. The head of Warrior A (left) retains not only its piercing eyes of ivory and colored stone and its silver teeth but also its copper eyebrows and lips, all inlaid after the magnificent statue was cast by some unknown sculptor about 460 BC.

FULFILLING THE DREAM OF A GREEK WORLD

The head of Heracles wrapped in a lion-skin adorns a silver vessel from the royal tombs of Vergina. As the reputed ancestor of Macedonian kings, Heracles' face displays the features of the Macedonian ruler Alexander the Great.

The Greek archaeologist Manolis Andronicos had to struggle to maintain a demeanor of cool professional detachment as he gently put down the golden box and opened it. Inside were cremated remains. But whose? "Our eyes nearly popped out of our sockets," he admitted later, recalling the emotions of the moment. "I moved a little apart from my colleagues on the excavation, the visitors and the police and stood alone to recover from that unbelievable sight. Everything indicated that we had found a royal tomb; and if the dating we had assigned to the objects was correct, as it seemed to be, then I did not even dare to think about it. For the first time a shiver ran down my spine, something akin to an electric shock passed through me. Had I held the bones of Philip in my hands? It was far too terrifying an idea for my brain to assimilate."

Philip II, as Andronicos knew, was one of antiquity's greatest figures. After assuming the Macedonian throne at the age of 23, Philip required only 4 years to transform his kingdom into one of the most powerful states in the Greek world and only 17 more years to become master of all Hellenes—including even the once-great Athenians. Yet the achievement that assured him a place in history was his fathering of the ancient world's most celebrated empire builder, Alexander the Great.

The burial site, a mound 360 feet in diameter known as the Great Tumulus, lay in a mountain-shadowed landscape near the Macedonian village of Vergina, about 30 miles north of Mount Olympus. Densely covered with the remnants of ancient greatness, the area contained some 300 burial mounds and the traces of a royal capital, with its palace, theater, and shrines. The site had first come to the attention of archaeologists in 1855, when a young French scholar by the name of Léon Heuzey, traveling through the region, learned of its existence as the result of a chance conversation with a local priest.

After his own brief but ill-fated excavations—cut short by a malaria epidemic among his diggers—Heuzey predicted that Vergina would one day yield spectacular secrets. "Within these Macedonian monuments, as in the subterranean tombs of Egypt and Etruria," he wrote, "there is more than a selection of ancient objects for us to recover; there lies the life and a history of an entire people awaiting our discovery."

Andronicos and his colleagues launched an excavation of the tumulus in late August of 1977. Within a few weeks the excavators made three important discoveries: the foundations of a building thought to be a heroön, or shrine dedicated to the worship of the dead; a tomb, plundered by graverobbers, bearing a fine wall painting of Pluto kidnapping the divine maiden Persephone; and most tantalizing of all, a second tomb, larger than the first one, sealed by two intact marble doors—the only pair to survive unbreached from the days of the ancient Greeks.

Positioned above these portals, on the facade of the sepulcher, was a painted frieze of extraordinary skill and sophistication depicting a hunting party in the process of dispatching a lion, a stag, some game birds, and other prey. "The size of this tomb," Manolis Andronicos wrote, "the sensational wall painting, taken together with the discovery of the 'small' tomb and the foundations of the Heroön, led us to think that this tomb must have belonged to an exceptionally important personage."

In November the team entered the burial chamber. To avoid damaging the doors, the excavators resorted to the tried-and-true

A young woman shrinks in fear in a detail from a still-vivid painting depicting the rape of Persephone that covers an entire wall in a Vergina tomb thought by some to be that of Philip II. This and two adjacent scenes are among the few remaining examples of large-scale fourth-century BC Greek wall painting.

methods of early graverobbers: They removed the last piece to be put in place during the tomb's construction—the so-called keystone at the apex of the arched ceiling. Andronicos knew the block rested on the vault's rear wall; it could be taken out without causing a collapse. Peering through this aperture, he saw a room crammed with heaps of precious grave goods. Their colors struck him first: the deep green patina of oxidized bronze, iron rusted to a reddish black, the sheen of old silver, fragments of wood blackened by fire and decay but sprinkled with tiny leaves of gold.

The shapes of the objects soon revealed themselves *(pages 149-157)*: beautifully crafted vessels for bathing and banqueting; a lamp stand; a large round cover for a shield; half a dozen spearheads; a sword; and a set of armor wrought to a standard worthy of a king, complete with a hinged breastplate trimmed with gold and a tall, crested helmet of a style known to be the hallmark of Macedonian warriors in the age of Philip and Alexander. A diadem of gilded silver, similar to one that had been worn by Alexander and his successors in ancient portraits, lay with them.

But all these treasures paled before the object that stood against the chamber's rear wall: a two-and-a-half-foot-square marble sarcophagus. Only after every detail of the discoveries made so far had been recorded and the appropriate technicians and conservators had been summoned did Andronicos allow its lid to be lifted. Inside rested another container—a case of pure gold topped with a 16-point star. The onlookers recognized this object as a larnax, a vessel for holding the charred bones of a cremated corpse.

Indeed, the bones that Andronicos now expected to find lay within it, accompanied by a heavy golden wreath composed of re-alistically carved oak leaves and tiny acorns. The bones had apparently been wrapped in a cloth dyed a deep purple, a color reserved for royalty; the dye had leached onto the bones as the fabric disintegrated, leaving dark blue stains. The sight called to Andronicos's mind Homer's description of the burial of Hector, the hero killed by Achilles in the Trojan War: According to the *Iliad,* Hector's comrades in arms "gathered the white bones and placed them in a golden urn, covering them over with soft purple robes."

Whoever had performed the final tribute to the occupant of the tomb now under excavation had either observed the same burial customs as Greeks of a long-bygone era or—perhaps more likely—reconstructed every detail from a piece of literature familiar to all educated speakers of Greek, including the members of Macedon's royal house. Alexander the Great, in particular, was known to be a devotee of Homer's works and—according to his chroniclers—always carried a copy of the *Iliad* in his baggage.

Andronicos acknowledged that such evidence as this offered an evocative hint, rather than firm proof, that the man in the tomb might bear some close connection with Alexander the Great—who himself was known to have been interred elsewhere. But as the finds within the tomb were collated and analyzed, the archaeologist began to feel ever more strongly that the burial was certainly that of a Macedonian monarch of the second half of the fourth century BC and very possibly that of Alexander's own father, Philip II.

Andronicos dated many of the artifacts within the tomb, and the materials used in its construction, to a period encompassing the life spans of Philip and Alexander. Among many other clues, he pointed out the strong resemblance between portraits found in the tomb—figures from the hunt scene painted on the facade, and 14 tiny heads, carved from ivory, that may have adorned a long-vanished piece of wooden furniture—and certain medallions and mosaics, surviving from ancient times, that have traditionally been identified as representations of the two Macedonian leaders.

Other discoveries appeared to confirm Philip's well-documented war wounds. On one of the ivory figures, for instance, Andronicos discerned a small scar over the right eyebrow, surmounting an apparently sightless eye. He knew that an arrow had struck Philip II in that eye during a battle in 354 BC. Later, a group of British researchers would analyze the skull bones of the corpse itself, extracted from the larnax, and conclude that the right eye socket had markings consistent with a wound made by an arrow.

Among the grave goods, the excavators had also found a pair of gilded greaves, sheaths of metal that protected a mounted warrior's lower legs. When these were examined, the left one was found to be shaped differently and almost an inch and a half shorter than the right. Andronicos wondered if this imbalance might conceivably reflect the two leg wounds that Philip had suffered during his career, leading to the limp mentioned by the orator Demosthenes, the historian Plutarch, and other classical writers.

Some of Andronicos's colleagues disputed the notion that the tomb might belong to Philip. They pointed out that the period to which the burial chamber dated also included the reign of another of

Philip II's three sons—Philip III Arrhidaeus. He was Alexander's successor to the Macedonian crown but hardly his brother's equal. According to historians of the age, he suffered from epilepsy and other disabilities. Physically weak, he is unlikely to have made use of the arms and armor that figured so conspicuously among the burial goods or to have enjoyed the vigorous outdoor pleasures that were memorialized on the facade.

Nevertheless, there were arguments against Philip's occupancy as strong as those against the tenancy by Arrhidaeus. The barrel-vaulted construction of the tomb, some scholars say, was an architectural innovation not introduced into Macedon until after Philip II's death, when Alexander's own engineers brought home the idea from Mesopotamia. The diadem too, they assert, was an Oriental badge of royal status copied by Alexander after encounters with Asian kings. And two saltcellars numbered among the grave goods were of a style not introduced until some 20 or 30 years after Philip's passing. Moreover, the odd sizing and shape of the greaves bore no provable relation to the position and location of Philip's leg wounds, as recorded in the literary sources.

To deepen the mystery further, the cremated occupant of the larnax was not the tomb's only resident. In an antechamber, the archaeologists found another gold larnax, containing the bones of a woman in her twenties,

This is the sight Manolis Andronicos beheld as he peered down into his discovery after he removed the keystone in the ceiling (above): *a marble sarcophagus, piles of funerary objects, a rusting cuirass, and closed doors blocking access to another room. At right, a drawing of the subterranean tomb shows the main burial chamber with grave goods strewn on the floor; the antechamber, containing a second sarcophagus; and the structure's imposing entranceway, flanked by half columns and adorned with a painted frieze.*

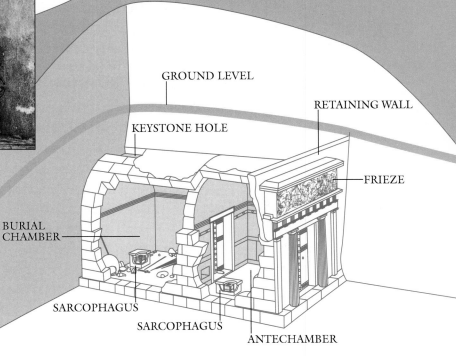

GROUND LEVEL

RETAINING WALL

KEYSTONE HOLE

FRIEZE

BURIAL CHAMBER

SARCOPHAGUS

SARCOPHAGUS

ANTECHAMBER

wrapped in two pieces of gold fabric adorned with purple branches, leaves, flowers, and spiral meanders. Her identity triggered even more furious debate. If the tomb did indeed belong to Philip II, was she one of his several wives, a favorite concubine, or the daughter of one of these liaisons? Scholars scoured the texts of this well-documented age to construct a detailed family tree and found half a dozen women who—by birth or marriage—enjoyed sufficiently high status to qualify for the honor of a royal burial.

Whoever she was, her grave goods included a set of armor for a female warrior, leading scholars to assume the occupant of the tomb was Queen Euridice, consort of the ailing Philip III Arrhidaeus. Macedon's own variety of Amazon, Euridice had been trained in the military arts and according to chroniclers had commanded the Macedonian army for a time. If the bones did belong to her, then it certainly would strengthen the case for Philip Arrhidaeus as the male occupant of the royal tomb.

The mystery remains unsolved and continues to tantalize. Scholars on both sides of the controversy still come up with proofs and counterproofs to challenge or confirm Andronicos's theory about the occupant of the kingly tomb. But whether the Philip in the chamber was the warrior-king who fathered Alexander or his sickly successor, members of both parties now agree that Vergina marks the probable site of the city of Aegae, Macedon's first capital and the traditional burial place for the members of its royal house.

And what is not in doubt is that the tomb itself, and the site where it lies, holds a rich trove of messages and mementos from Macedon's golden age, when it carried Greek civilization deep into the heart of Asia and brought back new ideas and images from the East. The process would be violent, and it would be swift, taking place largely within the short life spans of a pair of remarkable monarchs, Philip II and Alexander the Great. Yet the legacy of their conquests was the transformation of the old Hellenic civilization of Greece into something more complex and more cosmopolitan, which would shape the politics, culture, and daily life of the Mediterranean lands—and far beyond them—for centuries to come. The legacy of Alexander was the Hellenistic age, an era of intellectual expansiveness and artistic ferment that would last for some 300 years.

Within this timespan, great cities, founded by Alexander himself or his political heirs, would rise in Egypt, Asia Minor, and as far east as Afghanistan, where the civilization of Greece would reach out

Digging a shallow trench for a waterpipe in his garden in 1986, a Bulgarian villager was taken by surprise when he spotted the glint of buried treasure. Archaeologists called to the site from a nearby museum immediately began excavations, uncovering a total of 165 silver vessels—bowls, jugs, and cups dating from the fifth and fourth centuries BC, 31 of them gilded, and all identified as Thracian. Some are shown below.

Ancient Thrace lay east of Macedon in today's Bulgaria, bounded by the Aegean, Black, and Marmara Seas. Its tribes were known to the Greeks as early as the Bronze Age, when the Thracians proved their prowess as allies

126

of Troy against Mycenae. During that conflict, Homer noted in the *Iliad*, the king of Thrace wore gold armor worthy of the gods.

When Philip II launched his bid for domination of the region in 356 BC, he quickly overcame the politically fragmented Thracians and by 341 was their ruler. He took control of Thrace's mines, and the silver and gold they yielded filled his war chest. And, in another benefit of conquest, he brought under his command Thracian soldiers who would help Philip and his son Alexander realize their dreams of empire.

Archaeologists are not certain who buried this hoard, or why, but some suspect that local royals were trying to keep their family's wealth from falling into the hands of the Macedonians. If so, they must have become victims of the conquerors, since they never came back for their valuables.

and meet the ancient and equally sophisticated society of the Indian subcontinent. In their wake, the Macedonians and their successors—the Seleucid kings of Asia and the Ptolemies in Egypt—left the marks of their presence, ruined monuments that still retain an air of decayed magnificence. From the Balkans to the Hindu Kush, their tombs, temples, palaces, marketplaces, theaters, and fortresses have survived—sometimes in tantalizing fragments, sometimes in remarkable states of preservation—to capture the imagination and inspire the labors of generations of archaeologists.

The citizens of Athens and the other Hellenic city-states thought their northern neighbors strange, remote, and more than a little primitive. The Macedonians still cleaved to archaic tribal customs that southerners had long abandoned. They lacked experience in any form of democratic self-government, giving their loyalty to feudal chieftains who were ruled—uneasily—by kings. Historically, the fertile plains of Lower Macedon and the mountainous Upper Macedonian highlands had been controlled as four separate kingdoms, but the lowland kings of the Argead dynasty, Philip's forebears, had long regarded themselves as the overlords of their highland neighbors. The highlanders' own view of this relationship varied from one generation to the next, depending on the ability of the current Argead ruler to enforce his will.

The Argeads traced their ancestry to Heracles, the mythical superhero and strongman, fathered upon a mortal mother by the great god Zeus. The family awarded itself the epithet "Zeus-born," and Philip—who ascended the Argead throne in 359 BC—minted coins bearing images of Zeus and Heracles to remind the world of the Argead inheritance, in which godly powers merged with more-than-human strength. Much of what we know of the life of Philip comes from historians, such as Plutarch, writing some three or four centuries after Philip's death and taking their material from Greek documents now long since lost.

In the time-honored tradition of monarchs with troublesome neighbors, Philip used the marriage bed to cement alliances and consolidate power. He took five wives during his lifetime, not always waiting until one had died in childbirth before obtaining another. His contemporaries joked about the strategic timing of these marriages, remarking that Philip acquired a new wife for each new war.

127

The third of these consorts, however, proved more than a match for him. Olympias, a princess from the Molossian house of Epirus, an ancient kingdom straddling the present-day border of Albania and Greece, traced her own ancestry to the great hero of the Trojan War, Achilles. Barely 18 years old at the time of her marriage, she was not easily daunted by the prospect of power struggles with any of her polygamous husband's other consorts. In spite of fathering Alexander and a daughter, Cleopatra, upon her, Philip soon learned to keep a respectful distance from his Molossian queen. As well as possessing a forceful personality, Olympias was a passionate devotee of ancient mystery cults, familiar with potentially lethal spells and charms and particularly fond of snakes. Plutarch reports that Philip once entered her bed chamber, presumably with amorous intent, and found a very large serpent nestled cozily beside the sleeping queen; his ardor dampened, the king swiftly tiptoed out again.

But Philip's ambitions required him to make not only love but also war. In the spring of 356 BC, his troops crossed the Strymon River, Macedon's eastern boundary, into Thrace, and they occupied the rich mining district surrounding Mount Pangaeum, a seemingly inexhaustible source of gold and silver. With a powerful military presence to secure the region, and a large number of Macedonian settlers to work the mines, Philip minted the first regular gold coinage in the history of Europe (the coins of Athens were silver and bronze) and used it shrewdly.

Knowing well—as he is credited with saying—that no city was impregnable so long as an ass laden with gold could slip through its back gate, Philip spent part of the funds on diplomatic gifts and bribes to buy the loyalty of his nobles and the goodwill of foreign chieftains and kings. Other resources were directed toward Macedon's own development, to encourage the transition from a pastoral economy to one based on agriculture: Part of Lower Macedon, because of its lush, fertile soil, had long been known as the Gardens of Midas, after the legendary monarch with the golden touch, and Philip intended to exploit this fecundity. To improve internal communications and enhance the security of his realm, he built roads and fortresses and spurred the growth of cities as centers of trade.

The lion's share of Philip's profits went to the development of his army. He turned a band of volunteers and tribal warriors into a professional and well-equipped fighting force, bolstered by foreign warriors with particularly desirable skills. Macedonian noblemen formed Philip's cavalry, while hardy peasants and mountaineers armed with 14-foot-long *sarissas*—pikes measuring about twice the length of normal thrusting spears—provided an infantry amply equipped with grit and endurance.

Philip's own considerable military talents had been enhanced early, at a time when the city-state of Thebes, having defeated Sparta at Leuctra, in east-central Greece, in 371 BC, emerged as one of the most powerful states in Greece. Philip's older brother, then the ruler of Macedon, quickly negotiated an alliance with the Thebans and as a show of sincerity sent 15-year-old Philip as a diplomatic hostage.

Catapult ports top a finely constructed third-century BC masonry wall that once protected the frontier of Attica near Aigosthena, a city on the Gulf of Corinth. Though Greek fortifications became ever more elaborate to deter increasingly sophisticated battering rams and artillery, they still were vulnerable to determined infantry equipped with scaling ladders.

While enjoying this enforced hospitality, Philip had come into contact with the great Theban general Epaminondas, victor of Leuctra, and learned invaluable lessons on the most effective uses of different troops and the division of his forces into offensive and defensive wings. But once in command of his own armies, Philip soon outstripped his Greek neighbors, especially in the science of siegecraft, which the southerners had never perfected. And his opponents were shocked to discover that he was prepared to drive his troops into battle even during the winter, which had previously been a closed season, when warriors went home to mend their weapons and lie low.

After 358 BC Philip cut a swath through the entire region. Winning by military might what he could not gain by diplomacy, he fomented rebellion and dissension among the Greek city-states, harassed Athenian shipping in a long-running battle for all-important trade routes, and finally seized control of a huge tract of southeastern Europe, from the Black Sea to the Adriatic and from the Danube River southward to the Gulf of Corinth. In Athens, Demosthenes argued long and passionately for the city-states to join together against the Macedonians. But it was not until 339 BC, when Philip occupied Elatea, a town northeast of Mount Parnassus, thereby

129

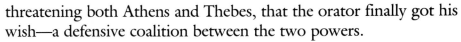

threatening both Athens and Thebes, that the orator finally got his wish—a defensive coalition between the two powers.

After a failed initial attempt to check the northerners' advance, the allies met Philip's forces in August 338 BC at Chaeronea, a city to the southeast of Parnassus. In the face of an opening Athenian assault, Philip, on the right wing, pretended to retreat, thinning the center of the Greek line, while Philip's 18-year-old son, Alexander, in command of the Macedonian cavalry, advanced on the left. When a gap finally opened in the Athenian ranks, Alexander's troopers raced through and turned on the heart of the Greek force—the crack Theban Sacred Band, the same infantry regiment that had helped crush the Spartans at Leuctra 33 years earlier. As the Thebans fell, the golden age of autonomous Hellenic city-states died with them.

Philip set himself up as the leader of a new confederacy of Hellenes, even though his erstwhile enemies would have disputed his right to membership in such a union. No longer were Macedonians to be marginalized and dismissed as not-quite-Hellenic outlanders; they now stood at the very center of power. As a mark of his new status, Philip decided that the time had come to unite all of Greece in an attack on an ancient enemy. In 336 BC he dispatched 9,000 foot soldiers and 1,000 cavalry across the Dardanelles and into Asia Minor, to challenge the might of the Persian Empire.

Before he could make his mark in the East, however, Philip found himself ensnared in a more intimate form of warfare within his

palace. For reasons of his own, Philip had obtained an additional wife, the daughter of the general in command of the Macedonian armies, and she soon was carrying his child. Olympias, worried about the implications for the inheritance of the throne by her son, Alexander, withdrew in an ominous mood. Philip then complicated matters by marrying off young Cleopatra, his daughter by Olympias, with the girl's own uncle, the Molossian king. The atmosphere at the wedding can only be imagined.

The nuptials were marked by prolonged festivities, including a day of competitive games in the theater at Aegae. Some 2,300 years later, Manolis Andronicos would uncover the exact site where these events took place. Excavating a trench almost 200 feet from the palace, he identified remnants of the curving walls of the auditorium's orchestra section, the first row of seats, the side corridors, and some of the foundations of the performance space itself. "It was," he wrote later, "a discovery so unbelievable that it might have almost deliberately been put in our way."

Yet any unseen forces of destiny that might have hovered about the spot, however helpful to the modern archaeologist, had been considerably less benevolent toward the ancient king. To launch the ceremonies, a grand procession of Macedonian nobles and warriors had escorted their royal master to the arena. Then Philip, eager to display his own invulnerability, commanded his bodyguards to stand back, while he, robed in purest white, strode alone into the theater and acknowledged the wild applause of the crowd.

At that moment, a young guardsman by the name of Pausanias rushed up to the monarch and ran him through with a sword, then bolted from the theater. As blood darkened the dying king's snowy garments, several young Macedonian nobles dashed out after the assassin. Pausanias made it through the city gates before he tripped over the gnarled root of an old grapevine and was pierced by the javelins of his pursuers.

Even as the avengers pulled their weapons from the killer's corpse, rumors began to fly through the city and the court. It was whispered that Pausanias had once had a love affair with the king, who was not averse to liaisons with his own sex in between his heterosexual couplings. But members of a more knowledgeable inner circle implied that while Pausanias had been the one who wielded the weapon, unseen enemies may have been hovering at his elbow, waiting for the blade to do its work. Suspicion fell, predictably, upon the

A fierce-visaged, 18-foot-tall stone lion (far left) commemorates the valor of the Theban Sacred Band, a group of warriors, in the pivotal battle of Chaeronea in 338 BC. Erected soon after Philip's victory over the Thebans, the statue was restored in 1903 by Greek Archaeological Society workers, seen at left around the new base. The lion, still in pieces on the ground, originally sat within a precinct containing the common grave of 254 slain members of the Sacred Band.

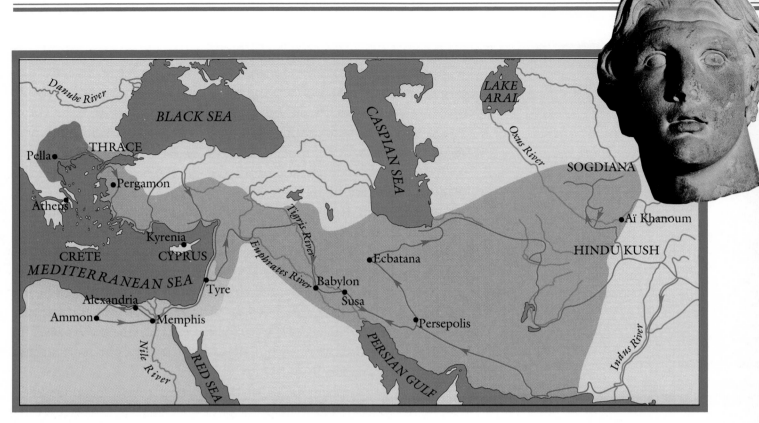

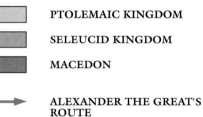

malcontent Molossian queen. "Most of the blame," Plutarch reported, "devolved upon Olympias." Whether she had taken an active part in a murder plot or used her reputed occult powers to steer Philip toward some unspecified evil end or simply stood back and hoped for his eventual comeuppance, Olympias had her revenge. And, more significant for the history of half the world, her son, Alexander, at 20 years of age already a seasoned veteran of diplomatic missions and military campaigns, now stood ready to succeed—and ultimately to surpass—his illustrious father.

Alexander's public and private lives are well documented, thanks to the efforts of such Roman-era biographers as Plutarch, Diodorus Siculus, and especially Arrian, who in the second century AD was still able to consult extant—and now lost—copies of memoirs by Alexander's intimates: his general Ptolemy; the military engineer Aristobulus; the admiral Nearchus, who was also a boyhood friend of the ruler's. Illustrations in mosaics, sculpture, and coins have even preserved a good idea of Alexander's appearance—expressive gray eyes, a clean-shaven complexion, a mane of wavy blond hair, and a prominent forehead.

The young king seems to have liked artists and felt at ease with them. He was on intimate terms with the most celebrated painter of

PTOLEMAIC KINGDOM

SELEUCID KINGDOM

MACEDON

ALEXANDER THE GREAT'S ROUTE

Alexander the Great, seen above in a supposed likeness from Pergamon in today's Turkey, subdued some of the greatest cities of Asia Minor and Asia in his fourth-century BC campaign of conquest. This map traces his route. After his death in 323, without benefit of his extraordinary vision, the empire he had created failed to hold together. By 275 parts had already been lost and the remaining portion carved into three separate kingdoms.

his age, Apelles, and paid frequent visits to the artist's studio. To the great amusement of apprentices preparing the colors, Alexander would hold forth—sometimes with stunning ignorance—on the finer points of artistic technique. To Apelles, it was said, the king eventually gave the exclusive right to paint his portrait, and he conferred the equivalent privilege on the sculptor Lysippus. A Roman copy of one of these statues, believed to be a faithful likeness of the original piece, still survives.

But even from portraits of the most dubious provenance, the intelligence of the royal sitter shines through. His father, Philip, never one to miss an opportunity to maximize resources, hired Aristotle, who was an old boyhood friend and one of Plato's best students, as young Alexander's tutor. When the philosopher received the summons to the Macedonian court, he was pursuing his pioneering works in the natural sciences, philosophy, rhetoric, and poetics in Mytilene, on the Aegean island of Lesbos, where he had settled following Plato's death.

The prince's wits, fostered by Aristotle's teaching, must have been sharp. Many chroniclers tell the tale of how the young Alexander tamed a horse named Bucephalus, which had proved too wild for even the most seasoned riders in his father's court. Some onlookers may have suspected that the boy had inherited his mother Olympias's alleged penchant for casting spells, but the truth was less alarming: Alexander had observed that the horse panicked at the sight of its own shadow and pacified the animal by turning it to face into the sun. Whether their bond had been cemented by magic or merely by sensible handling, Alexander and his mount entered into a long-lasting partnership that would become the stuff of legend.

A prince schooled by the world's greatest writer on the subject of logic could hardly help but acquire a hardheaded approach to obstacles. Once, about to engage in battle at a dangerous river crossing, he faced a near-mutiny by his senior officers. Reluctant to admit their fears—of the treacherous terrain and of a fight they considered unwinnable—his commanders reminded him that this was the month of May, a time when Macedonian kings traditionally abstained from fighting. More interested in victory than in kowtowing to hoary superstitions, Alexander snapped, "In that case, we'll have April all over again!" and led the cavalry charge himself.

He was a young man in a hurry. Philip had set the agenda for Asian conquest, and Alexander resolved to carry it out. By the end of

BRINGING BACK TO LIFE A CARGO SHIP THAT SAILED IN THE AGE OF ALEXANDER

Though hundreds of ancient shipwrecks litter the floor of the Aegean and Mediterranean Seas, they are not easy to locate. And whenever one is discovered, as happened in 1965 off Kyrenia on Cyprus, excavating it poses an enormous challenge. An alert Cypriot, out sponge diving, had spotted a pile of amphorae lying among eelgrass some 100 feet down (background). These almost certainly indicated a wreck, and as a resposible citizen, he informed underwater archaeologist Michael Katzev. When Katzev and his wife, Susan, dived to the site, they became convinced that

a ship indeed rested there. But how old might it be? Describing the shape of the amphorae to an expert, they got the answer: very old. Such amphorae dated from the fourth century BC.

Under the aegis of the University of Pennsylvania, the Katzevs and a team of excavators began the painstaking work of exposing and raising the wreck. First they had to remove the mat of vegetation. For this they used a sharp-ended instrument that

could be inserted into the mat to inject air under the roots and lift the weeds. Slowly, additional amphorae came to light. And while many were empty, others contained some 10,000 almonds from the cargo, hidden there by acquisitive octopuses.

When carbon dates for the ship's wood were compared to those for the nuts, they suggested that the vessel may have been in use for almost a century. Thought to have been built

Underwater archaeologists work within a grid of pipes laid out over the Kyrenia wreck (right). *The diver in the front uses an airhose to remove sediment. Timbers subjected to chemical treatment to preserve them received occasional ironing* (below) *in order to smooth bumps caused by the process.*

around 389 BC, it apparently sank some 20 years after Alexander the Great's death in 323.

Four sets of crockery indicated a crew of four. Had the vessel gone down in a storm, and had the men drowned? The discovery of rusted iron spearpoints under the wreck hinted at another fate: The ship may have been attacked by pirates, plundered, and scuttled, the crew sold into slavery.

Usually, little remains of such ancient vessels, but a blanket of fine sand had protected this one, preserving 60 percent of its hull and fittings. After being treated with polyethylene glycol, which firmed up the soft wood and conserved it, the surviving fragments could be reassembled *(right)*.

With knowledge of ancient Greek shipbuilding methods greatly expanded by the find, a replica of the vessel was constructed. In 1986 the new ship, called the *Kyrenia II,* sailed the 500 nautical miles from Cyprus to Athens, passing through three gales, in which the hull remained tight and dry.

Representing a triumph of underwater archaeology and modern preservation methods, the 46-foot-hull sits on display in Kyrenia. Five years were spent recovering its 5,000 pieces, treating and reassembling them. The 2,300-year-old vessel had been built from the outside in, the ancient shipwrights having used what is known as the shell-first technique, with the frame added inside after the planking had been built up.

336 BC, he had persuaded the league of Hellenic city-states to join the great onslaught against the Persians, under his supreme command. Slowed down by the need to pacify Thrace and Illyria, his troublesome northern neighbors, and to quell a bitter rebellion by the city-state of Thebes, he led his army into Asia Minor in the early spring of 334 BC. The ancient historians differ on the size of the force: it seems to have numbered between 30,000 and 40,000 infantry and 4,000 to 5,000 cavalry.

The great expedition also included artists, engineers, and scholars. Alexander was marching into a new world crammed with wonders; no opportunity of interpreting, appreciating, and recording these discoveries should be lost. Nor, in the midst of military adventures, would he neglect his own intellectual appetites. Alexander's baggage train included a whole library of literary, philosophical, and historical texts, and new reading matter was sent to him at frequent intervals.

Within four years, Alexander had conquered half the Persian Empire, which in this period extended as far westward as Phoenicia and Egypt. From Asia Minor to the banks of the Nile, local rulers loyal to Darius III, the Persian king, were beaten on the battlefield, besieged into submission, or coaxed into shifting their allegiance to Alexander. The Egyptians even saw fit to crown him as pharaoh in a solemn ceremony at Memphis, their 2,600-year-old former administrative capital, in November 332 BC. Watching Alexander devour great gobbets of his dominions, Darius made several attempts to sue for peace, but all were curtly rejected.

"In future," announced Alexander in one of his replies to the Persian ruler, "whenever you communicate with me, send to me as king of Asia; do not write to me as an equal, but state your demands to the master of all your possessions." Nevertheless, when Darius died at the hands of one of his own disgruntled vassals, Alexander pursued his enemy's murderer with the determined fury of an avenging angel across the wilderness of Turkestan, finally handing over the captured assassin for trial and execution by a Persian court.

Yet even the conquering hero could perpetrate deeds that were less than heroic. Plutarch and Arrian, whose versions of events do not always agree, both state that Alexander spent the winter of 330 BC in Persepolis, the ancient ceremonial capital of Persia, quartered in its magnificent palace. Then he held a drinking party to celebrate the arrival of the spring fighting season. During the festivities, one of the revelers—possibly the Athenian mistress of Alexander's general Ptolemy—suggested that it would be poetic justice for the partygoers to burn the building down. After all, when the Persians had invaded Greece 150 years earlier, they had destroyed the Acropolis at Athens; now, generations later, the Greeks could pay back their old foes in kind.

Alexander, so these versions of the story go, ignored the protests of one of his counselors, threw the first torch himself and allowed the Athenian lady to toss in the second. Then, wine cups in hand, the company left the building to watch the flames attack the walls adorned with rows of tribute bearers and courtiers and lofty columns. Other historians do not mention the party at all, but they confirm that the ultimate blame for the fire did lie with Alexander himself, who would—with hindsight—regret the vandalism as an ill-judged act for a man who wished the Persians to accept him not as an alien invader but as their own new king.

While the Persians mourned their lost Persepolis, Alexander pressed on. After marching to the ancient city of Ecbatana, about 400 miles to the northwest, he moved to the shores of the Caspian Sea and struck out eastward, skirting the northern borders of present-day Iran and Afghanistan, to the Hindu Kush—its mountain passes still cloaked in the last of the winter snows—and the northeastern Persian province of Sogdiana. Then, having consolidated his conquest of the Persian Empire, he turned south and entered the Indus Valley, where he prepared to invade the little-known kingdom lying beyond the river's far shore—India.

When he did so, in 327 BC, Alexander found himself pitched against all the obstacles that this extreme and extraordinary land could put in his way: monsoons, debilitating heat, and the troops of the rajah of Lahore, mounted upon 200 trumpeting elephants trained for battle. Yet none of these in the end defeated him. It was mutiny among his own soldiery that drove Alexander back to Persia, and still he left colonies behind him.

Even without a wholly subdued India to boast of, Alexander had plenty of outlets for his prodigious energies. No military leader had ever conquered such a huge spread of territory nor had such plans for the lands that he took. Alexander founded cities, fostered trade and improved public administration, built roads and harbors. He also encouraged the implantation of Greek culture in a very literal manner, by marrying his elite corps of officers to Persian ladies. His purpose, according to some historians, was to create a cosmopolitan blend of Eastern and Western civilization; other modern scholars contend that Greeks in Asia, like colonizers of more recent times, were less interested in exchanging ideas with their hosts than they were in creating a little replica of home on foreign soil.

But in Babylon on the morning of June 10, 323 BC, a few weeks short of his 33rd birthday, death took Alexander the Great. The cause of death remains a matter of some controversy. Poisoning was suggested, but later analysis of the medical evidence suggests that an infection—caused perhaps by an insect bite, contaminated water, or a wound gone septic—may be a likelier culprit. His death devastated his intimates and loyal subjects, but he had also made enemies who did not suppress their satisfaction at the ruler's early passing. "Alexander dead?" spat an Athenian orator. "Impossible. The whole world would stink of his corpse."

Yet most of the world, or so it seemed to those who witnessed these events, turned out to gape at the spectacular funeral carriage built to carry home the fallen conqueror. His corpse, embalmed in spices by specialists who had prayed for divine license "to handle the body of a god," rested in a golden coffin under a purple cloth embroidered with threads of gold. Still more gold glowed upon the miniature temple that crowned the catafalque, with its jeweled roof, Ionic columns, four statues of the trophy-bearing spirit of Victory, ibex heads, entwined acanthus leaves, and an olive wreath—all worked by smiths and master artisans in the same metal, bright and blinding in the desert sun.

A pattern of light and shadow emphasizes the graceful arches in this third-century theater cistern on the island of Delos. Ironically, the arch often went unseen in ancient Greece, where architects used it not to enhance the beauty of their buildings but only for support in underground or other hidden areas.

Large bells attached to the cornice of the moving shrine rang out to alert the waiting crowds to its coming. And to edify the onlookers, painted scenes in several panels illustrated highlights of the hero's career: Alexander in a state chariot, his cavalry ready for battle, files of Indian war elephants, a flotilla of ships. Even the wheels were gilded and decorated with golden lions bearing spears in their teeth. So too were the trappings of the 64 mules that pulled the great equipage out of Asia.

According to the customs of his ancestors, Alexander should have been interred at Aegae, the old Macedonian capital, in one of the royal tombs that would, far in the future, dazzle the eye of archaeologist Manolis Andronicos. But Alexander's faithful general Ptolemy—who had taken for himself the Egyptian portion of his master's empire—diverted the cortege to Egypt instead and buried the body at Memphis, where it lay in peace only until the late fourth or early third century BC. Then one of Ptolemy's descendants had the remains moved to Alexandria, a city that Alexander himself had founded, where it was reburied, only to be unearthed once more toward the end of the third century BC and placed in a communal mausoleum.

Here the body of Alexander the Great lay for some 300 years, in a sarcophagus of gold within a tomb that became a shrine. When another Ptolemy descendent melted down the golden coffin in 89 BC in order to fend off a fiscal disaster, the embalmed corpse—said to be still in perfect and beautiful condition—was transferred to a coffin somewhat more humbly decorated with colored glass. The tomb survived as a place of pilgrimage for centuries: Alexander's successors as well as Egypt's conquerors, Julius Caesar, Mark Antony, and Rome's first emperor, Augustus Caesar, all came to pay their respects.

Caracalla, emperor of Rome in the early third century AD, made the last recorded visit in 215. Shortly after that, Alexandria became the scene of violent riots, during which Alexander's tomb may have been damaged and looted. Further indignities no doubt occurred in the years to come, so that by the fourth century AD, no one could say for sure where Alexander's body lay. Locating it, of course, has long been a persistent goal of archaeologists. In fact, the Egyptian Antiquities Organization has logged more than 140 search-

es, including one as recent as 1991. Yet not one has turned up anything identifiable as a tomb.

No less mysterious were Alexander's intentions for what was to become of his great empire following his death, since he neither named an heir nor left any verifiable testament for the disposition of his vast dominions. When asked on his deathbed to whom he bequeathed his vast holdings, Alexander is said to have answered ambiguously. "To the strongest," he whispered. "I foresee a great funeral contest over me."

In the end, after much tortuous jockeying for power, the empire was carved up into three separate parts, each region ruled by descendants of Alexander's old comrades in arms: The heirs of Ptolemy controlled Egypt, forging a dynasty that would endure for more than 250 years. Macedon and Thessaly passed to the line of another general, named Antigonus. The Greek cities to the south, though they were once more officially independent, remained under the sway of their northern neighbors. Across the Aegean Sea, another of Alexander's senior officers, Seleucus, managed to forge most of conquered Asia into a single kingdom, although an Indian king, Chandragupta, won back those parts of his homeland that Alexander had taken. And while Ptolemies and Seleucids contended for control of such economic and strategic plums as southern Syria and the coast of Asia Minor, other eastern territories—including the one known as Bactria—slid out of Seleucid hands.

In the early 1960s an unusual item turned up in a small Afghani museum: an ancient stone capital adorned with two rows of carved acanthus leaves. The architectural style had originated some 3,000 miles to the west, in the Greek city of Corinth. Yet according to the owner of the Afghani museum, the capital had been discovered at the confluence of the Oxus and Kokcha Rivers, in a remote valley located about 200 miles north of Kabul. From the piece's great size, archaeologists knew immediately that it was a major find, for it offered hard proof not only of Greek settlement in the east but also of a major Hellenistic metropolis.

The discovery of Aï Khanoum, as the city was known, helped rewrite history. Ancient chroniclers had spoken of Greek towns flourishing in the remote central Asian region they called Bactria, but no archaeological evidence—apart from coins—had ever confirmed

High-stepping lions pull a cart bearing a winged goddess personifying Victory and Cybele, the Asian nature goddess adopted by the Greeks, on this plaque found in the ruins of a temple at Aï Khanoum in Afghanistan. Priests attend the goddesses as the sun god Helios, the moon, and a star fill the sky. The images and artistic style on the gilded silver disk show a remarkable fusion of cultures that occurred in this easternmost of Greek kingdoms.

In this photo of the Greek-held city of Aï Khanoum, the stepped podium of the largest of the city's three temples betrays no outward Greek influence (foreground). Although a sculpted sandaled foot found in the temple suggests its deity may have been wearing Greek dress, buried vessels indicate at least some rites performed there were not Hellenic in character. Behind the structure, a truck parked in the center of a palace courtyard conveys the enormous scale of the complex.

the existence of these colonies. In fact, some modern scholars had dismissed the notion of a Hellenistic civilization this far east as a "Greco-Bactrian mirage."

A 15-year excavation that was begun in 1965 and led by the French archaeologist Paul Bernard has proved the cynics to be wrong. The city of Aï Khanoum was founded either by Alexander himself, when he conquered the old Persian frontier province of Bactria, or by Seleucus, who made it a regional capital of his kingdom. In about 200 BC, however, Bactria seceded and became an independent Greek-ruled kingdom dominating a broad swath of territory—parts of present-day Pakistan, Afghanistan, Uzbekistan, Tadzhikistan, and Turkmenistan. Aï Khanoum remained one of its main centers until approximately 145 BC, when nomadic invaders from the north drove the Greeks out.

The French investigation of the site uncovered a royal palace of considerable grandeur. The enclosure extended over some 20 acres and featured a great colonnaded courtyard, public reception halls and private apartments, a warren of rooms that apparently housed government bureaucrats, and a treasury. In storage were inscriptions—in Greek—recording the receipt of Greek and Indian coins, as well as fragments of crystal, lapis lazuli, and precious gems, which are all that remain of the costly objects that were once held there. The archaeologists also discovered traces of a library containing Greek texts. The material on which these works were written had long since crumbled, but the ink remained, imprinted on the surfaces where the scrolls once lay. The Greek words were faint but just legible enough for the researchers to identify an essay in Aristotelian philosophy and some fragments of a poem.

Outside this royal complex lay a city bearing other hallmarks of the Greek culture and lifestyle of some—if not all—of its inhabitants. The excavation unearthed an upper-class residential district containing commodious houses equipped with mosaic-tiled bathrooms; the decorations were firmly in the Greek tradition, even if the tiling techniques themselves seemed decidedly old-fashioned in comparison to those employed by contemporary artisans back home. The community also boasted amenities that would not have been out of place in any Hellenistic city-state: an open-air theater seating several thousand spectators; a gymnasium adorned with the customary Greek tributes to Hermes and Heracles as patrons of the physical training that took place there; and monumental funerary steles, in-

cluding one engraved with the last five of a famous series of maxims displayed upon Apollo's shrine at far-off Delphi, expounding the moral attributes of the ideal Greek. "In childhood," they say, "learn good manners; in youth learn to control your passions; in middle age learn to be just; in old age learn to be of wise counsel; die without regret."

Plutarch had long ago claimed that in the easternmost provinces colonized by the Greeks, Alexander had left in his wake a land whose inhabitants could read Homer and recite the plays of Sophocles and Euripides. It now seemed that an ancient historian not always relied upon for accuracy might, in this instance, be speaking simple truth. Indeed, the form and content of the surviving texts indicated that the colonists of Aï Khanoum, despite the great distance that separated them from the mother country, took pains to ensure that their children learned Greek grammar, spelling, and penmanship of a standard equal to anything spoken or written in the Mediterranean area.

Some scholars, analyzing the findings at Aï Khanoum, suggest that a rampart lining the banks of the city's rivers and an imposing city wall may have separated the Greek colonists from the indigenous population. A similar barrier was thought to have existed, and served the same purpose, thousands of miles to the west of Aï Khanoum, in present-day France, where Greeks had founded the city of Marseilles. But there were also signs that the colonists, despite their preference for all things Greek, were not entirely immune to local influences. In a temple within the royal complex, for instance, excavators turned up a gilded silver plaque whose imagery mingles Oriental and Greek elements.

It seems unlikely, however, that many of the Greek colonists in Aï Khanoum or its counterparts elsewhere in Bactria or India turned so wholeheartedly away from their own culture as did Menander, who ruled over a Hellenistic enclave in western India between about 155 and 130 BC. Intense conversations with a Buddhist priest named Nagasena had persuaded him of the truths to be found in this Eastern faith. Coins from his royal mint bore images of the Greek goddess of wisdom, Pallas Athena, but other relics of his reign are stamped with the Eastern symbol of the Wheel of Law.

Sea creatures, real and imaginary, border a star in a mosaic that decorated the floor of one of the Aï Khanoum palace bathrooms. Elite baths in the city were quite elaborate, frequently divided into separate rooms for dressing, heating water, and bathing.

Only bases remain along the southern colonnade of the Aï Khanoum palace's main courtyard. Drums of the fallen columns line the wall at top left. Holes originally dug around each of the bases supported scaffolding used by the builders to erect the courtyard's 116, 30-foot-tall columns, which were topped with Corinthian capitals.

Indian chroniclers gave him the Sanskrit name Milinda, remembering him as a saint and the builder of many Buddhist shrines. Upon Menander's death, his Indian subjects divvied his ashes between the chief cities of his kingdom.

If the outermost rim of the Hellenistic universe lay beyond the Hindu Kush, at Aï Khanoum and other stubbornly Greek enclaves, its center—according to many scholars—could be found not in Greece itself but in the great city of Alexandria, located on Egypt's Mediterranean coast. Here, in 331 BC, Alexander himself paced the slender strip of land that lay between the sea and Lake Mareotis. Accompanied by his architect Deinochares, Alexander marked out the perimeters for a new city, planning the location of agora and temples, angling the grid of streets to take advantage of cool breezes off the water. Its founder's aspiration, claimed the chronicler Aristander, was to create a great urban center that would be a "nursing mother to men of every nation."

Standing where European, Asian, and African worlds converged, Alexandria could hardly be anything but international. Its diverse communities—indigenous Egyptians, Hellenes, a large and well-established colony of Jews—may not have intermingled any more than the exigencies of civil and commercial life required, but they gave the city a cosmopolitan air that would endure for more than 2,000 years. After Alexander's death, the Ptolemies would rule the city—and all of Egypt—as their private fiefdom; like despots everywhere, they milked the profits of urban trade and rural agriculture for their personal gain. Yet they also channeled a portion of this wealth into two ambitious intellectual enterprises.

The first of these projects was the museum, an institution of higher learning, offering the leading scholars of the day free board and lodging and a pleasant, cloistered environment—of covered arcades, shady recesses, quiet seats—where they might pursue their intellectual adventures. Although 72 Jewish scholars translated the Septuagint, the five books of Moses, from Hebrew into Greek under its auspices, the museum's intellectual bias remained emphatically Greek; the indigenous Egyptian culture was apparently regarded, at best, as something peripheral and exotic by those who looked to the Hellenic world for their cultural heritage.

The Hellenistic city of Pergamon, in a watercolor below by 19th-century architect and artist Richard Bohn, is seen as it might have looked at its height in the second century BC, its famed Great Altar visible to the theater's right. In the 1879 photo at left, German engineer Carl Humann (second from left) and the dig's sponsor, Alexander Conze (center), pose with Bohn and others in front of a work shack bearing the name of the ships, the Loreley *and the* Comet, *that carried pieces of the altar to Germany. At bottom, another 19th-century watercolor shows the site after initial excavations.*

The second scholarly institution became the stuff of legend, even in its own time. This was the Great Library of Alexandria, dedicated to the preservation of every known work of Greek literature, in every discipline, lest the wisdom of the ancients be lost or forgotten. Vast resources were poured into the enterprise in order to acquire a collection that, at its peak, numbered some half million scrolls. To help build up the archive, Ptolemy III passed a law requiring every ship that put in to port at Alexandria to hand over any manuscripts on board to be copied. The library, however, kept the originals; only the duplicates were returned to the manuscript owners.

In the pursuit of particularly important works, Ptolemy and his chief librarian did not feel bound by an excess of moral scruples in their dealings with others. When the city of Athens, for instance, reluctantly loaned out its precious official texts of the dramas of Aeschylus, Sophocles, and Euripides, it insisted that the Alexandrians first pay a hefty sum as security. Once the Ptolemy of the day knew that these treasures had arrived, he decided to let the Athenians keep the money and held on to the scrolls. But not all the resources of the Ptolemies could protect this repository forever: During a Roman attack on Alexandria in the first century BC, a fire consumed this irreplaceable collection.

The Ptolemies, however, were not the only Hellenistic kings aspiring to intellectual glories. By the early second century BC, the Attalids, a dynasty that rose to power in the northwestern corner of Asia Minor, possessed a capital city of their own, Pergamon, that they hoped might rival Alexandria in greatness. They too built a library, whose resident scholars began making their own bids for texts, scribes, and copyists in all corners of the Greek-speaking world.

The Alexandrians did not welcome the competition in what had previously been a buyer's market and duly enacted a ban on exporting papyrus, hoping that—without this essential material for the manufacture of scrolls—the upstarts would be stopped in their tracks. The resourceful inhabitants of Pergamon retaliated by inventing, from dressed sheepskin or goatskin, a far more popular medium for the copying of texts. Its name, parchment, derives from the Latin word for the city that devised it.

Located on the site of present-day Bergama, Turkey, about 20 miles inland from the Aegean shore, Pergamon in its heyday had been

THE SAGA OF THE PERGAMON ALTAR

Walking into the main hall of Berlin's Pergamon Museum, a visitor encounters a second-century BC religious monument of spectacular proportions and artistry, which suffered and survived the vicissitudes of World War II. Sixty-foot-wide marble steps ascend to a stately colonnade, flanked by sculptures depicting a mythic battle between gods and giants. So lifelike are the writhing figures that they partly stand and lie on the steps.

The exhibit, a re-creation of part of Pergamon's Great Altar, incorporates elements from the almost 400-foot-long marble frieze unearthed by Carl Humann in Turkey in the late 1800s and transported to Berlin in 97 large slabs and 2,000 smaller fragments. Not satisfied with displaying isolated pieces of what one classicist called "the climax of Greek sculpture," museum officials undertook a massive restoration of the western section of the altar. In doing so, they had to ignore the criticisms of people who objected to the placement of the ancient sculptures in a modern replica of the Greek structure. Undaunted, the Germans went ahead, even erecting a special museum to house the finished assemblage.

Then came World War II, the Allied bombing of Berlin, and the battle for the city. Museum officials had removed all the original portions for safekeeping, but the victorious Soviets carried them off to Leningrad. In 1959, in a gesture of goodwill to Communist Germany, Nikita Krushchev had the pieces returned to East Berlin. After conservators tended to the altar, which had been damaged by the strife, the museum reopened its doors. Today, the rebuilt Great Altar of Pergamon remains a supreme example of the majestic grandeur of Hellenistic sculpture as well as, noted a curator, "a monument to museology."

At left, workers repair the war-damaged altar. The museum's reconstruction (below) represents only one-third of the original altar.

a splendid sight. The Attalid acropolis stood upon a mountain soaring 1,000 feet above the coastal plain. In the Hellenistic manner, its royal architects displayed a penchant for ornate decoration and construction on the grandest of scales. Fifteen hundred years later, a visiting Byzantine prince—the future emperor Theodore II Lascaris—confessed himself humbled by its earthquake-broken remains. "It is full everywhere of the majesty of the Hellenic spirit," he wrote. "Walls rise up no less high than the brazen heaven, great in artistry. These could never be the work of hands, or the conception that of a modern mind: they astonish the onlooker!"

But most astonishing of all was a monument that this royal tourist never saw, for the tremors that destroyed the city in the Middle Ages also shattered the Great Altar of Zeus, with its massive and powerfully detailed relief of the war between the gods and the giants. It had been one of the ancient world's most talked about wonders and was, according to biblical scholars, the very Throne of Satan named in the Book of Revelation. But it seemed to have been lost for all time until its rediscovery, virtually by chance, at the hands of a 19th-century German engineer named Carl Humann.

Humann had originally come to the Aegean island of Samos, about 100 miles to the south, for his health and became interested in the ruins of Pergamon while he was engaged in road-building projects for the Ottoman Empire. In 1871 he observed that an old Byzantine wall on the acropolis of the ruined city incorporated fragments of a much more ancient frieze. These he removed and sent to the Berlin Museum, which expressed little interest in any further excavation of the site.

In 1878, however, a newly appointed director of the museum's sculpture collection, a man by the name of Alexander Conze, realized the possible implications of Humann's finds. Conze immediately sent word to Humann, urging him to launch a hunt for the celebrated altar. After a lifetime's experience on construction sites, Humann was able to make an educated guess as to the altar's likely location. He knew exactly how far the Byzantine wall builders might have been prepared to go in search of useful fragments to recycle.

Noting the presence of a mound of debris in a promising spot, Humann drafted a small brigade of workers to help him and began to dig. Within three days, the Great Altar had come to light. Some of the reliefs were in remarkably good condition,

147

with many figures of battling gods and giants still virtually intact. "We have found a whole epoch of art," Humann wrote to his Berlin sponsors. "The greatest work to have survived from antiquity is here beneath our hands."

Removing such a masterpiece from Asia Minor, however, required a combination of persuasion, hard cash, and a bit of trickery, for the Ottoman government demanded that two-thirds of the finds remain in the country. After considerable negotiation, the Turks eventually dropped this requirement in exchange for 20,000 marks from the German government, but Humann still had some of his 97 marble slabs and 2,000 frieze fragments packed facedown for good measure. That way, he figured, Turkish customs officials would see nothing more than the blank reverse of the stone slabs. Back in Berlin, where the Great Altar was restored and reconstructed *(page 146)*, he was feted as a national hero.

The Attalid kings who had created this celebrated monument enjoyed only a brief spell of glory. By 133 BC the last Pergamene king had bequeathed his realm to Rome, whose leaders, in the manner of the unforgotten Alexander, now looked hungrily toward the East. The Attalids' old rivals, the Ptolemies, would survive for another century before they too would fall. The last of the dynasty founded by Alexander's trusted general was Cleopatra, queen of Egypt. Despite her best efforts to deflect the Roman onslaught—her legendary liaisons with Julius Caesar and Mark Antony were more likely to have been inspired by political pragmatism rather than romantic love or simple lust—Egypt too became a Roman province, in 30 BC. Four years later, all of Greece would follow. ⊠

A GOLDEN PAYOFF

Forty years would go by before the Greek archaeologist Manolis Andronicos made the discovery that had eluded him much of his professional life. As a student, working in northern Greece on the ruins of a third-century BC palace, Andronicos grew familiar with the archaeologically rich area. But World War II intervened, shutting down the dig, and the Greek Archaeological Service did not assign Andronicos to the region until after the conflict. In 1952 he sunk his first trench into a large burial mound known as the Great Tumulus, convinced it concealed an important tomb. But cutting more than 20 feet down into the 40-foot-high, 360-foot-diameter pile of dirt produced nothing of significance. Without proper funding to proceed, the archaeologist turned to smaller mounds.

A decade later, Andronicos tried again. Opening an even bigger trench, more than 115 feet long, 50 feet wide, and 38 feet deep in the Great Tumulus, he unearthed only fragments of marble tombstones. Could the elusive tomb lie below the mound? he speculated. Yet another 13 years elapsed before he could attempt an answer. He began by removing a portion of the mound—40 tons of soil in all. In 1977, having reached ground level, Andronicos had five test trenches dug, all to no avail. On the sixth try, workers uncovered a crude wall. Find soon followed find: the burned bones of a sacrifice, fourth-century BC pottery, another wall, an empty tomb, then stone slabs covering a subterranean vault, and finally a columned facade with marble doors. After entering the structure through the roof, he found himself inside a burial chamber with relics strewn about, among them the ivory miniature above; the features so fitted descriptions of Philip II that Andronicos wondered if this could be the king's tomb. The identity of the charred bones Andronicos found there in a gold box may never be firmly established, but the tomb yielded enough extraordinary objects to indicate that it was indeed the final resting place of royalty.

A gilded quiver leans against the marble entryway between the antechamber and the main burial chamber (left). In front of it are a pair of greaves, or leg armor, and alabaster ointment jars. The antechamber, its walls still a vivid red, held a sarcophagus containing the bones of a young woman carefully wrapped in gold-threaded purple brocade.

In the corner behind the quiver, Andronicos found what remained of its contents, 74 arrowheads and their decomposed wooden shafts. The arrowheads were of three sizes, more appropriate for hunting than for battle.

An intricate relief believed to depict the capture of a city, with soldiers brandishing swords and shields and frightened maidens fleeing, embellishes the quiver. An unusual item for a Macedonian tomb but similar to others found in southern Russia, the quiver may have been booty taken in combat with the Scythians, fierce riders of the Eurasian steppes.

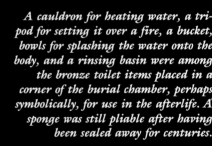

A cauldron for heating water, a tripod for setting it over a fire, a bucket, bowls for splashing the water onto the body, and a rinsing basin were among the bronze toilet items placed in a corner of the burial chamber, perhaps symbolically, for use in the afterlife. A sponge was still pliable after having been sealed away for centuries.

A bronze lamp holder adorned with the face of the goat-god Pan stood among the water vessels. Perforated with many small holes, it not only would have allowed light to shine through but also would have kept the lamp from being extinguished by a splash. Upright, looped handles permitted it to be carried.

Bits of gold and ivory and a heap of disintegrated organic material (left) littered the floor behind the large round bronze object leaning against the wall in the photograph opposite. Andronicos believed at first that the disk was a shield, but when he peered behind it he realized it was merely a shield cover. Reconstruction of the badly decayed ceremonial showpiece, fashioned from wood and leather and decorated with gold and ivory, took nearly five years (below); it includes an ivory image of a man and a woman.

The goddess Athena, protector of Macedon, graces the front of an iron helmet, part of an elaborate set of warrior's accouterments sealed away in the burial chamber. The first Macedonian helmet ever found, it sports a distinctive crest and decorative laminated designs on both the brow and cheek pieces.

Its shoulder pieces rusted almost beyond recognition, a soldier's iron and leather cuirass, or body armor, lies in pieces on the floor in the middle of the tomb, where it is thought to have landed after the bench on which it presumably sat collapsed. Gold ornaments in the shape of lions' heads can be seen beside the remains.

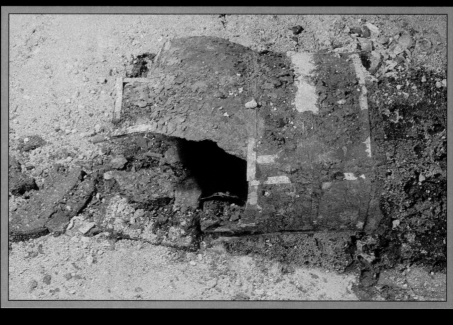

Expecting to open the burial chamber's plain marble sarcophagus (right) *and find a funerary urn inside, Andronicos gasped at the sight of the solid-gold larnax, or casket, below. The 13-by-16-by-7-inch larnax bore a large embossed star burst, the Macedonian royal emblem, as well as blue-glass rosettes and other floral designs. Carefully washed bones, tinted over time by the purple cloth in which they had been wrapped, nestled alongside a wreath of gold oak leaves* (bottom).

A STIRRING ASCENT TO GREATNESS

EARLY PERIOD
1050-750 BC

ARCHAIC PERIOD
750-500 BC

GEOMETRIC KRATER

ARCHAIC KOUROS

Following the final collapse of the literate Mycenaean culture, the last of the glorious Aegean Bronze Age civilizations, mainland Greece and the islands off its shores entered what some historians call a dark age. This term, however, more accurately describes the dearth of historical information concerning the interval beginning around 1050 BC rather than a lack of skills or knowledge among the inhabitants, although writing was lost. In fact, it was during this period of transition into the Iron Age that the political, esthetic, and literary features of classical Greek civilization began to appear. Local leaders calling themselves kings ruled over small, tightly knit communal groups, which presaged Greece's city-states. Painted pottery took on a distinctly new aspect, its form simpler but more solid, while its design, as evidenced by the vessel in the geometric style above, exhibited a new elegance, harmony, and proportion, all hallmarks of later Greek art. Borrowing from the hazily remembered history of the Mycenaeans, the Trojans, and others who had come before, itinerant bards wove tales of gods and humans that gave poetic shape to Greek mythology. Toward the end of this era, Greek-speaking people appropriated the alphabet of the Phoenicians and adapted it to their own language, permitting the transcription of their many longstanding oral traditions, the best of which survive as Homer's epics, the *Iliad* and the *Odyssey*. With this return to literacy, Greek prehistory ended, and the traditional date of the first Olympic Games, 776 BC, marked the beginning of a henceforth unflagging Greek cultural ascendancy.

In the eighth century, increases in population and prosperity caused waves of Greek emigrants to seek new agricultural land and trading opportunities throughout the Mediterranean area. Greek settlements in foreign lands were not just satellites of their founding cities, however, but separate, autonomous political entities. The independent spirit that motivated the settlers, plus the collective action needed to sustain each community, produced the political unit that was the polis. In all, it is estimated that there were as many as 700 such city-states in the Greek world. Foreign cultures contacted during this period of expansion influenced the Greeks in many ways. Geometric pottery decoration surrendered to Eastern-style images of animals and swirling free-form designs as well as detailed scenes from mythology in the innovative black-figure style of vase painting. Artists began working in stone, clay, wood, and bronze to produce monumental sculptures of humans. A typical archaic statue, the kouros above reveals an obvious debt to Egyptian art but also possesses an incipient flair for symmetry, lightness, and realism. The first true Greek temples appeared in the seventh century, decorated with continuous friezes and columns in Doric style. Lyric and elegiac poetry, both personal and emotional, supplanted the more stately verse of the past. Intensified commerce promoted the widespread use of the Lydian invention of coinage. On the mainland, Sparta adopted a political system emphasizing rigorous control and discipline, enabling it to become the largest and most powerful city-state of the time. In contrast, Athens reformed and codified its laws to promote justice and equality, opened its ruling councils to more citizens, and laid a foundation for democracy.

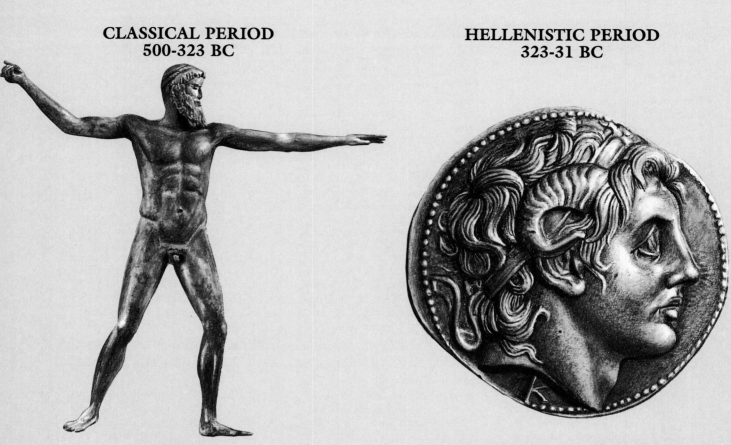

CLASSICAL PERIOD
500-323 BC

HELLENISTIC PERIOD
323-31 BC

BRONZE ZEUS

SILVER COIN WITH ALEXANDER'S HEAD

The classical period of Greece, an explosive efflorescence of art, literature, philosophy, and politics, was bracketed by major conflicts with two foreign powers, Persia and Macedon. The Greek victory over Persia engendered a newfound spirit of cooperation among the various city-states, with Athens, whose fleet had turned the tide against the so-called barbarians, taking a leading role. Contributions from the allies to Athenian coffers in return for military protection enabled the city to amass still greater wealth and pursue political, cultural, and economic hegemony throughout the Mediterranean. Virtually all Athenian citizens, regardless of their financial status, became eligible for public office and were paid a stipend for their service. Publicly funded sculptors, architects, and dramatists produced works that remain triumphs of human achievement. The seven-foot-tall bronze statue of Zeus above, for example, epitomizes the classical Greek mastery of the human form captured with extraordinary dynamism. Greek philosophers, historians, and scientists set the standard for rational, theoretical analysis. In 431 the longstanding rivalry between Athens and Sparta erupted into a war lasting nearly 30 years, ending with the fall of Athens. Years of fighting left a vacuum of leadership within many of the city-states, and bitter disputes continued to arise. The shrewd and ambitious king of Macedon Philip II took advantage of the chaotic situation and soon became master of all Greece. Philip's empire building halted with his assassination and the ascension to the throne of his son Alexander. Only 12 years later, Alexander the Great died, leaving behind an empire that stretched from the Adriatic into India.

After nearly 50 years of wrangling over succession, three major powers arose from the ashes of Alexander's empire: Macedon, Ptolemaic Egypt, and the Seleucid territory, which extended from Turkey to Afghanistan. Amazingly, from Macedon's Pella in the West to Aï Khanoum in the East, the language, literature, political institutions, art, architecture, and philosophy of the cities and settlements that had sprung up in Alexander's wake retained their intrinsic Greekness. Successor kings emphasized their connections with Greece, particularly with Alexander, who is portrayed on the silver Thracian coin above wearing the horns of Zeus Amon, a god with both Eastern and Western ties. With a common language and the influence of trade, written texts, and travelers, the Hellenistic world grew more and more cosmopolitan. Education and literacy flourished, and libraries—among them the Great Library in Alexandria, Egypt, with some half a million volumes—proliferated. But the Greek ruling classes refused to admit subjects into their inner circles, and the huge, sprawling kingdoms suffered constant battering from internal revolts. Macedon, increasingly weakened and impoverished, fell to Rome in 168 BC. One by one, local Seleucid governors declared independence, forming many, smaller dynastic polities. Egypt, ruled by the Ptolemies, was the last holdout of Alexander's successor kingdoms. Cleopatra VII, the final Ptolemaic ruler and the only one to learn the language of her dominion, committed suicide after the Roman victory at Actium. Roman mastery of the Mediterranean world did not signal the end of Greek influence, though, for the Romans embraced Greek culture and perpetuated the Hellenic legacy as even the Greeks were unable to do.

ACKNOWLEDGMENTS

The editors wish to thank the following individuals and institutions for their valuable assistance in the preparation of this volume:

Bernard Andreae, Instituto Archeologico Germanico, Rome; Nadir Avci, Ministry of Culture, Ankara; John Bastias, Ekdotike Athenon S.A., Athens; Paul Bernard, Ecole Normale Supérieure, Paris; Jacklyn Burns, The J. Paul Getty Museum, Malibu, California; Jane Carter, Tulane University, New Orleans; Joseph C. Carter, University of Texas, Austin; Elipida Chairi, Ecole Française d'Archéologie, Athens; Kalliopi Christofis, Ecole Française d'Archéologie, Athens; Anastasia Chrysochoidou, Hellenic Republic Ministry of Culture, Athens; John Coates, Bath, England; Brian Cook, London; Stella Drougou, Vergina Excavations, Thessaloniki, Greece; Finmeccanica, Rome; Ellen Fladger, Union College, Schenectady, New York; Klaus Goldmann, Staatliche Museen zu Berlin–Preussischer Kulturbesitz, Museum für Vor- und Frühgeschichte, Berlin; Michael H. Jameson, Stanford University, Stanford; Ian Jenkins, British Museum, London; David Jordon, Gennadius Library, Athens; Jan Jordon, Agora Excavations, American School of Classical Studies, Athens; Klaus Junker, Deutsches Archäologisches Institut, Berlin; Ursula Kästner, Staatliche Museen zu Berlin–Preussischer Kulturbesitz, Antikensammlung, Berlin; Volker Kästner, Staatliche Museen zu Berlin–Preussischer Kulturbesitz, Antikensammlung, Berlin; Michael Katzev, Arlington, Vermont; Heidi Klein, Bildarchiv Preussischer Kulturbesitz, Berlin; Emre Kongar, Ministry of Culture, Ankara; Donna Kurtz, Beazley Archive, Ashmolean Museum, Oxford; John Morrison, Cambridge; Chrysoula Paliadell, Vergina Excavations, Thessaloniki, Greece; Alpay Pasinli, Istanbul Archaeological Museum, Istanbul; Jerry Podany, The J. Paul Getty Museum, Malibu, California; C. Martin Robertson, Cambridge; Eva Rystedt, Medelhavsmuseet, Stockholm; Ori Z. Soltes, Klutznick Museum, Washington, D.C.; Anna Tuteur, A.C.T., Milan; K. V. von Eickstedt, Deutsches Archäologisches Institut, Athens; Hafed Walda, Ashmole Archive, Kings College, University of London, London; Elizabeth Wayward, British School in Athens, London; Chris Williams, University of Texas, Austin; Penny Wilson, British Archaeological School, Athens.

PICTURE CREDITS

Unknown Artist, Kouros (detail, torso, ultraviolet), 530-520 BC, Thasian? marble—Collection of the J. Paul Getty Museum, Malibu, California, Unknown Artist, Kouros (detail, magnification of surface alteration crust), 530-520 BC, Thasian? marble. 64, 65: Mimmo Jodice, Naples—foto: Claus Hansmann, Munich. 66, 67: Staatliche Museen zu Berlin–Preussischer Kulturbesitz, Antikensammlung, foto: Ingrid Geske-Heiden. 69: Foto: Claus Hansmann/The Metropolitan Museum of Art, New York. 70, 71: Staatliche Museen zu Berlin–Preussischer Kulturbesitz, Antikensammlung; Ekdotike Athenon S.A., Athens/National Archaeological Museum, Athens. 72: Hubert Josse, Paris/courtesy Musée Municipal Antoine-Vivenel, Comiègne; Badisches Landesmuseum, Karlsruhe, Germany. 74, 75: By permission of the Master and Fellows of Corpus Christi College, Cambridge; Martin von Wagner/Museum der Universität Würzburg Antikenabteilung. 76, 77: H. L. Pierce Fund, courtesy Museum of Fine Arts, Boston; © British Museum, London. 78, 79: Staatliche Museen zu Berlin–Preussischer Kulturbesitz, Antikensammlung, foto: Johannes Laurentius; Ashmolean Museum, Oxford. 80: Staatliche Museen zu Berlin–Preussischer Kulturbesitz, Antikensammlung, foto: Johannes Laurentius. 81: © Erich Lessing, Culture and Fine Arts Archive, Vienna/Kunsthistorisches Museum, Antikensammlung, Vienna. 82: National Archaeological Museum/Archaeological Receipts Fund TAPA service, Athens. 86-88: American School of Classical Studies at Athens: Agora Excavations. 89: © British Museum, London. 90-93: American School of Classical Studies at Athens: Agora Excavations. 94: Art by John Drummond, Time-Life

Books, based on the drawing by John Coates in *The Trireme Project,* edited by Timothy Shaw, Oxbow Monograph 31, 1993; Nan Shaw, Gloucester. 95: The Trireme Trust/photo: Paul Lipkeme. 96: Robert L. Vann. 97: Courtesy the Istanbul Archaeological Museum, photo by Turahan Birgili—© Sonia Halliday Photographs, Weston Turville, Bucks, England. 99: Ecole des Beaux Arts, Paris. 100, 101: © David Levenson, Surrey; Timm Rautert/Visum Archiv, Hamburg. 102, 103: © David Levenson, Surrey. 104-106: American School of Classical Studies at Athens: Agora Excavations. 108, 109: Foto: Heaton/Schapowalow, Hamburg. 111-119: Background by Larry Sherer. 111: Eric Brissaud/Gamma, Paris. 112, 113: National Archaeological Museum/Archaeological Receipts Fund TAPA service, Athens. 114, 115: Nimatallah/Ricciarini, Milan/National Archaeological Museum, Athens; National Archaeological Museum/Archaeological Receipts Fund TAPA service, Athens. 116: Fulvio Rizzo, Reggio Calabria; Soprintendenza Archeologica della Toscana, Florence. 117: Eric Brissaud/Gamma, Paris—Soprintendenza Archeologica della Toscana, Florence. 118: Liberto Perugi, Florence/Museo Archeologico, Reggio Calabria. 119: Nimatallah/Ricciarini, Milan/Museo Archeologico, Reggio Calabria(2). 120: Studio Kostas Kontos, Athens/Archaeological Museum of Thessaloniki. 122: Ekdotike Athenon S.A., Athens/Archaeological Museum of Thessaloniki. 125: The Greek Ministry of Culture and Sciences, Athens; art by John Drummond, Time-Life Books, based on a drawing in *Vergina: The Royal Tombs,* by Manolis Andronicos, Ekdotike Athenon S.A., 1984. 126, 127: Vladimir Vitanov

Agency, Sofia, Bulgaria. 129: Ekdotike Athenon S.A., Athens. 130: Deutsches Archäologisches Institut, Athens/courtesy Dr. K. V. von Eickstedt; Deutsches Archäologisches Institut, Athens. 132: Map by John Drummond, Time-Life Books; Silvio Fiore/Explorer, Paris. 134, 135: Michael L. Katzev, Arlington, Vermont, except lower left by Susan Womer Katzev, Arlington, Vermont. 138, 139: Robert L. Vann. 140-143: Paul Bernard. 144, 145: Staatliche Museen zu Berlin–Preussischer Kulturbesitz, Antikensammlung—Archiv für Kunst und Geschichte/Pergamon Museum, Berlin—Ecole des Beaux Arts, Paris. 146, 147: Staatliche Museen zu Berlin–Preussischer Kulturbesitz, Antikensammlung. 149: Archaeological Museum of Thessaloniki/Archaeological Receipts Fund TAPA service, Athens. 150: Ekdotike Athenon S.A., Athens/Archaeological Museum of Thessaloniki. 151: Ekdotike Athenon S.A., Athens/Archaeological Museum of Thessaloniki—Archaeological Museum of Thessaloniki/Archaeological Receipts Fund TAPA service, Athens. 152, 153: Ekdotike Athenon S.A., Athens/Archaeological Museum of Thessaloniki (top 2)—Archaeological Museum of Thessaloniki/Archaeological Receipts Fund TAPA service, Athens (bottom 2). 154: Ekdotike Athenon S.A., Athens/Archaeological Museum of Thessaloniki. 155: Archaeological Museum of Thessaloniki/Archaeological Receipts Fund TAPA service, Athens. 156, 157: Archaeological Museum of Thessaloniki/Archaeological Receipts Fund TAPA service, Athens (2), except top and bottom left Ekdotike Athenon S.A., Athens/Archaeological Museum of Thessaloniki. 158, 159: Art by Paul Breeden.

BIBLIOGRAPHY

BOOKS
Anderson, Patrick. *The Smile of Apollo: A Literary Companion to Greek Travel.* London: Chatto & Windus, 1964.
Andronicos, Manolis:

Delphi. Athens: Ekdotike Athenon S.A., 1992.
National Museum. Athens: Ekdotike Athenon S.A., 1990.
"The Royal Tombs at Vergina: A Brief Account of the Excavations."

In *The Search for Alexander,* edited by Betty Childs. Boston: Little, Brown, 1980.
Vergina: The Royal Tombs and the Ancient City. Athens: Ekdotike Athenon S.A., 1984.

Archibald, Zofia. *Discovering the World of the Ancient Greeks*. New York: Facts On File, 1991.

Austin, M. M. *The Hellenistic World from Alexander to the Roman Conquest*. Cambridge: Cambridge University Press, 1981.

Bacon, Edward (ed.). *The Great Archaeologists*. Indianapolis: Bobbs-Merrill, 1976.

Bérard, Claude, et al. *A City of Images*. Translated by Deborah Lyons. Princeton: Princeton University Press, 1989.

Bernard, Bruce. *Photodiscovery: Masterworks of Photography, 1840-1940*. New York: Harry N. Abrams, 1980.

Bieber, Margarete. *Alexander the Great in Greek and Roman Art*. Chicago: Argonaut, 1964.

Biers, William R. *The Archaeology of Greece: An Introduction* (rev. ed.). Ithaca: Cornell University Press, 1987.

Boardman, John:
Greek Art (rev. ed.). London: Thames and Hudson, 1985.
The Greeks Overseas: Their Early Colonies and Trade. London: Thames and Hudson, 1980.
The Parthenon and Its Sculptures. Austin: University of Texas Press, 1985.

Boardman, John, Jasper Griffin, and Oswyn Murray (eds.):
The Oxford History of the Classical World. Oxford: Oxford University Press, 1986.
The Oxford History of Greece and the Hellenistic World. Oxford: Oxford University Press, 1991.

Branigan, K. (ed.). *The Atlas of Archaeology*. New York: St. Martin's Press, 1982.

Brinton, Crane, John B. Christopher, and Robert Lee Wolff. *A History of Civilization* (Vol. 1). New York: Prentice-Hall, 1955.

Brommer, Frank. *Die Parthenon-Skulpturen*. Mainz: Philipp von Zabern, 1979.

Browning, Robert (ed.). *The Greek World: Classical, Byzantine and Modern*. London: Thames and Hudson, 1985.

Camp, John M. *The Athenian Agora: Excavations in the Heart of Classical Athens*. New York: Thames and Hudson, 1986.

Canfora, Luciano. *The Vanished Library*. Translated by Martin Ryle. Berkeley: University of California Press, 1990.

Casson, Lionel. *The Greek Conquerors* (Treasures of the World series). Alexandria, Va.: Stonehenge Press, 1981.

Ceram, C. W. (ed.). *Hands on the Past: Pioneer Archaeologists Tell Their Own Story*. New York: Schocken, 1973.

Charbonneaux, Jean, Roland Martin, and François Villard. *Hellenistic Art, 330-50 B.C.* Translated by Peter Green. New York: George Braziller, 1973.

Christopoulos, George A. (ed.). *The Archaic Period* (History of the Hellenic World series). University Park: Pennsylvania State University Press, 1975.

Clayton, Peter A., and Martin J. Price. *The Seven Wonders of the Ancient World*. New York: Dorset Press, 1989.

Collier's Encyclopedia. New York: Macmillan Educational, 1982.

Cook, B. F. *The Elgin Marbles*. London: British Museum Press, 1991.

Cotterell, Arthur (ed.). *The Encyclopedia of Ancient Civilizations*. London: Penguin Books, 1980.

de la Croix, Horst, and Richard G. Tansey. *Gardner's Art through the Ages*. New York: Harcourt Brace Jovanovich, 1986

Desborough, V. R. d'A. *The Greek Dark Ages*. London: Ernest Benn, 1972.

A Dictionary of Ancient Greek Civilisation. London: Methuen, 1970.

Dinsmoor, William Bell. *The Architecture of Ancient Greece: An Account of Its Historic Development*. New York: W. W. Norton, 1975.

Douskou, Iris. *Athens: The City and Its Museums*. Athens: Ekdotike Athenon S.A., 1986.

Drower, Margaret S. *Flinders Petrie: A Life in Archaeology*. London: Victor Gollancz, 1985.

Empires Ascendant (TimeFrame series). Alexandria, Va.: Time-Life Books, 1987.

Encyclopedia of World Art. New York: McGraw-Hill, 1966.

Etienne, Roland, and Françoise Etienne. *The Search for Ancient Greece*. New York: Harry N. Abrams, 1992.

Finley, M. I. (ed.). *Atlas of Classical Archaeology*. London: Chatto & Windus, 1977.

Fol, A., B. Nikolov, and R. F. Hoddinott. *The New Thracian Treasure from Rogozen, Bulgaria*. London: British Museum Publications, 1986.

Fox, Robin Lane. *The Search for Alexander*. London: Allen Lane, 1980.

Garland, Robert. *The Greek Way of Life: From Conception to Old Age*. Ithaca: Cornell University Press, 1990.

Grant, Michael:
The Classical Greeks. New York: Charles Scribner's Sons, 1989.
The Founders of the Western World. New York: Charles Scribner's Sons, 1991.
The Rise of the Greeks. New York: Charles Scribner's Sons, 1987.
The Visible Past: Greek and Roman History from Archaeology, 1960-1990. New York: Charles Scribner's Sons, 1990.

Grant, Michael (ed.). *Greece and Rome: The Birth of Western Civilization*. New York: Bonanza Books, 1986.

Green, Peter:
Alexander of Macedon, 356-323 B.C. Berkeley: University of California Press, 1991.
Alexander the Great. New York: Praeger, 1970.
Alexander to Actium. Berkeley: University of California Press, 1990.
Classical Bearings: Interpreting Ancient History and Culture. London: Thames and Hudson, 1989.
The Parthenon. New York: Newsweek Books, 1973.
"The Royal Tombs at Vergina: A Historical Analysis." In *Philip II, Alexander the Great and the Macedonian Heritage,* edited by W. Lindsay Adams and Eugene N. Borza. Washington, D.C.: University Press of America, 1982.

Gulick, Charles Burton. *The Life of the Ancient Greeks*. New York: Cooper Square Publishers, 1973.

Hamblin, Dora Jane. *Pots and Robbers*. New York: Simon and Schuster, 1970.

Hambourg, Maria Morris, et al. *The Waking Dream: Photography's First Century*. New York: Metropolitan Museum of Art, 1993.

Hampe, Roland, and Erika Simon. *Un Millénaire d'Art Grec, 1600-600*. Fribourg: Office du Livre, 1980.

Harris, H. A. *Greek Athletes and Athletics*. Bloomington: Indiana University Press, 1966.

Holloway, R. Ross. *The Archaeology of Ancient Sicily*. London: Routledge, 1991.

Hopper, R. J.:
The Acropolis. London: Weidenfeld and Nicolson, 1971.
Trade and Industry in Classical Greece. London: Thames and Hudson, 1979.

Houser, Caroline. *Greek Monumental Bronze Sculpture*. London: Thames and Hudson, 1983.

Jacquemin, Anne. "En Feuilletant le *Journal de la Grande Fouille*." In *La Redécouverte de Delphes*. Paris: Ecole Française d'Athènese, 1992.

Jones, J. Ellis. "Laurion: Agrileza, 1977-83: Excavations at a Silver-Mine Site." In *Archaeological Reports for 1984-85*. Athens: Council of the Society for the Promotion of Hellenic Studies and the Managing Committee of the British School at Athens, 1985.

Kagan, Donald. *Botsford and Robinson's Hellenic History*. New York: Macmillan, 1969.

Karageorghis, Vassos:
Cyprus: From the Stone Age to the Romans. London: Thames and Hudson, 1982.
Salamis in Cyprus: Homeric, Hellenistic and Roman. London: Thames and Hudson, 1969.

Karl, Friedrich, and Eleonore Dörner. *Von Pergamon zum Nemrud Dag*. Mainz: Philipp von Zabern, 1989.

Kounas, Dionysios A. (ed.). *Studies on the Ancient Silver Mines at Laurion*. Lawrence, Kans.: Coronado Press, 1972.

Kunze, Max. *The Pergamon Altar*. Mainz: Philipp von Zabern, 1991.

Lacey, W. K. *The Family in Classical Greece*. London: Thames and Hudson, 1968.

Lawrence, A. W. *Greek Architecture* (rev. ed.). London: Penguin Books, 1983.

Levi, Peter. *The Cultural Atlas of the World: The Greek World*. Alexandria, Va.: Stonehenge Press, 1990.

Ling, Roger. *The Greek World* (Making of the Past series). New York: Peter Bedrick Books, 1988.

Lissarrague, François. *The Aesthetics of the Greek Banquet: Images of Wine and Ritual*. Translated by Andrew Szegedy-Maszak. Princeton: Princeton University Press, 1987.

MacKendrick, Paul. *The Greek Stones Speak* (2nd ed.). New York: W. W. Norton, 1981.

Mattusch, Carol C. *Greek Bronze Statuary: From the Beginnings through the Fifth Century B.C.* Ithaca: Cornell University Press, 1988.

Miller, Helen Hill. *Sicily and the Western Colonies of Greece*. New York: Charles Scribner's Sons, 1965.

Morrison, J. S., and J. F. Coates. *The Athenian Trireme: The History and Reconstruction of an Ancient Greek Warship*. Cambridge: Cambridge University Press, 1986.

Mussche, H. F. *Thorikos: A Guide to the Excavations*. Brussels: Comité des Fouilles Belges en Grèce, 1974.

Neils, Jenifer. "Goddess and Polis." Catalog. Hanover, N.H.: Hood Museum of Art, Dartmouth College, 1992.

The New Encyclopædia Britannica (Vol. 19). Chicago: Encyclopædia Britannica, 1984.

Nichols, Roger, and Kenneth McLeish (trans. and comps.). *Through Greek Eyes: Greek Civilisation in the Words of Greek Writers* (rev. ed.). Cambridge: Cambridge University Press, 1991.

Osborne, Robin. *Classical Landscape with Figures: The Ancient Greek City and Its Countryside*. London: George Philip, 1987.

Paris, Rome, Athenes: Le Voyage En Grèce des Architectes Français Aux XIX et XX Siècles. Houston: The Museum of Fine Arts, 1983.

Past Worlds: The Times Atlas of Archaeology. Maplewood, N.J.: Hammond, 1988.

Pedley, John Griffiths:
Greek Art and Archaeology. New York: Harry N. Abrams, 1993.
Paestum: Greeks and Romans in Southern Italy. London: Thames and Hudson, 1990.

Petrie, W. M. Flinders. *Ten Years' Digging in Egypt, 1881-1891*. Piccadilly: Religious Tract Society, 1893.

Plutarch. *The Rise and Fall of Athens: Nine Greek Lives*. Translated by Ian Scott-Kilvert. Baltimore: Penguin Books, 1960.

Pollitt, J. J. *The Art of Ancient Greece: Sources and Documents*. Cambridge: Cambridge University Press, 1990.

Pomeroy, Sarah B. *Goddesses, Whores, Wives, and Slaves: Women in Classical Antiquity*. New York: Schocken Books, 1975.

Pope, Maurice. *The Ancient Greeks: How They Lived and Worked*. Chester Springs, Pa.: Dufour Editions, 1976.

Renault, Mary. *The Nature of Alexander*. New York: Pantheon, 1975.

Robinson, C. E. *Everyday Life in Ancient Greece*. Oxford: Clarendon Press, 1933.

Rolley, Claude. *Greek Bronzes*. Translated by Roger Howell. London: Sotheby's, 1986.

Shaw, Timothy (ed.). *The Trireme Project: Operational Experience 1987-90/Lessons Learnt*. Oxford: Oxbow Books, 1993.

Snodgrass, Anthony M. *An Archaeology of Greece: The Present State and Future Scope of a Discipline*. Berkeley: University of California Press, 1987.

A Soaring Spirit (TimeFrame series). Alexandria, Va.: Time-Life Books, 1987.

Stoneman, Richard:
Across the Hellespont: A Literary Guide to Turkey. London: Hutchinson, 1987.
Land of Lost Gods: The Search for Classical Greece. Norman: University of Oklahoma Press, 1987.

Stoneman, Richard (trans.). *The Greek Alexander Romance*. London: Penguin Books, 1991.

Tatton-Brown, Veronica (ed.). *Cyprus BC: 7000 Years of History*. London: British Museum Publications, 1979.

Themelis, Petros G. *The Delphi Museum*. Athens: Ekdotike Athenon S.A., 1981.

Throckmorton, Peter (ed.). *The Sea Remembers: Shipwrecks and Archaeol-*

ogy. New York: Weidenfeld & Nicolson, 1987.

Tomlinson, Richard. *The Athens of Alma Tadema*. Wolfeboro Falls, N.H.: Alan Sutton, 1991.

Toynbee, Arnold J. *Twelve Men of Action in Graeco-Roman History*. Boston: Beacon Press, 1952.

Travlos, John. *Pictorial Dictionary of Ancient Athens*. New York: Praeger, 1971.

Trippett, Frank, and the Editors of Time-Life Books. *The First Horsemen* (Emergence of Man series). New York: Time-Life Books, 1974.

Tsigakou, Fani-Maria:
The Rediscovery of Greece. New Rochelle, N.Y.: Caratzas Brothers, 1981.
Through Romantic Eyes. Alexandria, Va.: Art Services International, 1991.

Twain, Mark. *The Innocents Abroad*. New York: New American Library, 1966.

Underwater Archaeology: A Nascent Discipline. Paris: UNESCO, 1972.

Vanishings (Library of Curious and Unusual Facts series). Alexandria, Va.: Time-Life Books, 1990.

Vickers, Michael. *Greek Vases*. Oxford: Ashmolean Museum, 1982.

Walker, Barbara G. *The Woman's Encyclopedia of Myths and Secrets*. San Francisco: Harper & Row, 1983.

Warry, John. *Warfare in the Classical World*. London: Salamander Books, 1980.

Waywell, G. B. *The Free-Standing Sculptures of the Mausoleum at Halicarnassus in the British Museum*. London: British Museum Publications, 1978.

Westwood, Jennifer (ed.). *The Atlas of Mysterious Places*. New York: Weidenfeld & Nicolson, 1987.

Wheeler, Margaret. *History Was Buried: A Source Book of Archaeology*. New York: Hart, 1967.

Williams, Dyfri. *Greek Vases*. Cambridge: Harvard University Press, 1985.

Wondrous Realms of the Aegean (Lost Civilizations series). Alexandria, Va.: Time-Life Books, 1993.

Woodford, Susan. *The Parthenon*. Cambridge: Cambridge University Press, 1986.

The World of Athens: An Introduction to Classical Athenian Culture. Cambridge: Cambridge University Press, 1984.

Wycherley, R. E. *The Stones of Athens*. Princeton: Princeton University Press, 1978.

Zimmern, Alice. *The Home Life of the Ancient Greeks*. Translated by H. Blümner. New York: Cooper Square, 1966.

PERIODICALS

"The Acropolis: Fighting Pollution." *Newsweek*, April 12, 1982.

"Acropolis: Threat of Destruction." *Time*, January 31, 1977.

Alsop, Joseph. "Warriors from a Watery Grave." *National Geographic*, June 1983.

Andronicos, Manolis. "Is This the Tomb of Philip of Macedon?" *National Geographic*, July 1978.

Bass, George F. "Classical Archaeology: The Great Tradition Looks Ahead." *Archaeology*, January/February 1989.

Bernard, Paul. "An Ancient Greek City in Central Asia." *Scientific American*, January 1982.

Bianchi, Robert S. "Hunting Alexander's Tomb." *Archaeology*, July/August 1993.

Bordewich, Fergus M. "What Are They Doing to the Parthenon?" *Traveler*, December 1988.

Felbermeyer, Johannes. "Sperlonga: The Ship of Odysseus." *Archaeology*, April 1971.

Fleischman, John. "In Classical Athens, a Market Trading in the Currency of Ideas." *Smithsonian*, July 1993.

Green, Peter. "Greek Gifts?" *History Today*, June 1990.

Hamblin, Dora Jane. "Italy's Marvelous Marble Jigsaw Puzzle with 20,000 Pieces." *Smithsonian*, February 1973.

Harrington, Spencer P. M. "Shoring Up the Temple of Athena." *Archaeology*, January/February 1992.

Henneberg, Maciej, Renata Henneberg, and Joseph Coleman Carter. "Health among the Ancient Greeks, Metaponto, Southern Italy, 600 to 250 BC." *Research & Exploration*, Autumn 1992.

Jackson, Donald Dale. "Lord Elgin's Greek Tragedy." *Smithsonian*, December 1992.

Jenkins, Ian. "James Stephanoff and the British Museum." *Apollo*, March 1985.

Katzev, Michael:
"Resurrecting the Oldest Known Greek Ship." *National Geographic*, June 1970.
"Voyage of Kyrenia II." *INA Newsletter*, March 1989.

Katzev, Michael, and Susan Katzev:
"Kyrenia II." *INA Newsletter*, November 1986.
"Last Port for the Oldest Ship." *National Geographic*, November 1974.

Linn, Alan. "Once Again Athens' Acropolis Finds Itself in Terrible Trouble." *Smithsonian*, March 1982.

Meisler, Stanley. "After the Wall: A National Treasure Is Rediscovered." *Smithsonian*, October 1991.

Murray, William. "Letter from Sperlonga." *New Yorker*, March 30, 1987.

Pearce, Ann. "Heroic Bronzes of Fifth Century B.C. Regain Old Splendor." *Smithsonian*, November 1981.

Pierce, Kenneth M. "Saving the Crumbling Parthenon." *Time*, October 3, 1983.

Popham, Mervyn, E. Touloupa, and L. H. Sackett. "The Hero of Lefkandi." *Antiquity*, November 1982.

Rensberger, Boyce. "Evidence of Ill Health Erodes Legend of Ancient Colony's Well-Being." *Washington Post*, November 16, 1992.

Scarre, Chris. "A Tomb to Wonder at." *Archaeology*, September/October 1993.

Schoder, Raymond V. "Ancient Cumae." *Scientific American*, December 1963.

"Silver Lining." *Discover*, March 1993.

Snodgrass, Anthony M., and John L. Bintliff. "Surveying Ancient Cities." *Scientific American*, March 1991.

Szegedy-Maszak, Andrew. "Picturing the Past." *Archaeology*, July/August 1989.

Toufexis, Anastasia. "The Glory That Was Greece." *Time*, August 17, 1987.

OTHER SOURCES

Buitron-Oliver, Diana. "The Greek

Miracle: Classical Sculpture from the Dawn of Democracy—The Fifth Century B.C." Catalog. Washington, D.C.: National Gallery of Art, 1992.

"The Greek Miracle." Brochure. Washington, D.C.: National Gallery of Art, 1992.

"The Human Figure in Early Greek Art." Catalog. Washington, D.C.: National Gallery of Art, 1988.

Karageorghis, Vassos, et al. "Cypriote Antiquities in the Medelhavsmuseet, Stockholm." Stockholm: Medelhavsmuseet, 1977.

"Kyrenia II: An Ancient Ship Sails Again." Pamphlet. Piraeus, Greece: Hellenic Institute for the Preservation of Nautical Tradition, 1987.

Ober, Josiah, and Charles W. Hedrick (eds.). *The Birth of Democracy: An Exhibition Celebrating the 2500th Anniversary of Democracy.* Catalog. Athens: American School of Classical Studies at Athens, 1993.

Oehser, Paul H., John S. Lea, and Nancy Link Powars. "The Submerged Sanctuary of Apollo at Halieis in the Argolid of Greece." Report. Vol. 14. Washington,

D.C.: National Geographic Society, 1973.

"The Pantanello Necropolis, 1982-1989." Report. Austin: University of Texas, 1990.

"The Search for Alexander." Catalog. Boston: New York Graphic Society, 1980.

Szegedy-Maszak, Andrew. "A Modern Look at Ancient Greek Civilization." Video. Dubuque, Iowa: The Teaching Company, 1992.

Vickers, Michael. "Greek Symposia." London: Joint Association of Classical Teachers, 1976.

INDEX

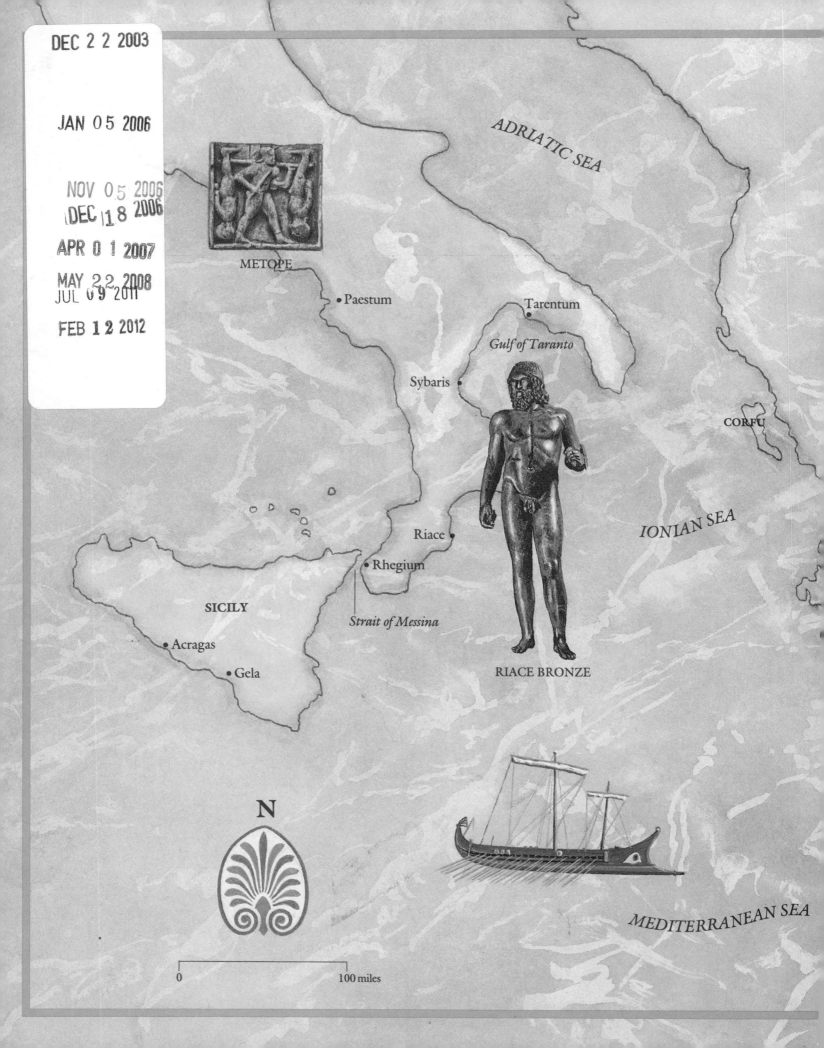

ADRIATIC SEA

METOPE

• Paestum

Tarentum •

Gulf of Taranto

Sybaris •

CORFU

Riace •

• Rhegium

Strait of Messina

IONIAN SEA

SICILY

• Acragas

• Gela

RIACE BRONZE

N

MEDITERRANEAN SEA

0   100 miles